Mastering Magic

100 Secrets of the Great Magicians

Mastering Magic

100 Secrets of the Great Magicians

by
Walter B. Gibson

LIFETIME BOOKS, INC.
2131 Hollywood Blvd., Suite 305
Hollywood, FL 33020

Library of Congress Cataloging-in-Publication

Gibson, Walter Brown, 1897-_
    Mastering magic : 100 secrets of the great magicians / by Walter B. Gibson.
        p.   cm.
    Includes index.
    ISBN 0-8119-0825-9 (pbk.)
    1. Conjuring--Juvenile literature. [1. Magic tricks.]
I. Title.
GV1548.G52   1994
793.8--dc20
                                                    94-44352
                                                        CIP
                                                         AC

Manufactured in the United States of America

1 2 3 4 5 6 7 8 9 0

Contents

Foreword ix

CHAPTER 1. CLOSE-UP MAGIC 1
  1. Coin and Saucer 3
  2. Dimes and Pennies 4
  3. Power of Thought 6
  4. Drop the Match-Box 7
  5. Card and Glass 8
  6. Glass and Cigarette 10
  7. Match in Mid-Air 11
  8. Three-Coin Twizzler 13
  9. The Twizzle Card 15
 10. One-Hand Knot 18
 11. Coin and Bottle 20
 12. The Puzzling Label 20
 13. Catch-the-Sugar 21

CHAPTER 2. POCKET MAGIC 25
  1. The Penetrating Match 26
  2. Stack-the-Chips 27
  3. Three Medals 29
  4. The Mysterious Domino 30
  5. Jumping Rubber Band 31
  6. Bottle and Pills 33
  7. Self-Opening Matchbox 34
  8. Self-Closing Matchbox 35
  9. Magnetized Glasses 36
 10. The Passing Pennies 37
 11. Three Divining Rods 38
 12. The Rattle Bars 39

CHAPTER 3. CARD TRICKS **41**
 1. Guess Again 42
 2. Find Your Own.. 44
 3. As Many as You 46
 4. The Double Clock.. 49
 5. Three-Deal Prediction 51
 6. Color Sense.. 53
 7. Faces Up 55
 8. Sure-Win Poker Hand 57
 9. The Identical Cards.. 58
 10. Nine-Card Deal 61

CHAPTER 4. PLATFORM MAGIC **63**
 1. The Quick-Change Handkerchief 64
 2. The Wandering Milk.. 65
 3. The Penetrable Card 67
 4. Modern Vanishing Glass.. 70
 5. The Vanishing Ink 71
 6. Adhesive Milk 74
 7. Bottle and Rope.. 76
 8. The Red Ribbon Pack 77
 9. Disecto.. 80
 10. The Patriotic Liquids 83
 11. The Penetrating Liquid 86
 12. The Vanishing Candle 87
 13. Card, Seal and Ribbon 88
 14. Sands of Sahara 90

CHAPTER 5. MYSTICISM **93**
 1. The Spirit Answer.. 96
 2. The Polar Ghost.. 97
 3. The Talking Key.. 98
 4. The Spooky Weights 99
 5. The Floating Table 101
 6. In the Dark 103
 7. Under Cover 104
 8. Catch the Ghost 107
 9. The Spirit Post 108
 10. Seance in the Light 112
 11. The Hand of Cagliostro 114

12. Cassadaga Propaganda 117
13. The Knotty Spook 000
14. The Clutching Hand 122

CHAPTER 6. STAGE ILLUSIONS 123
1. The Flowing Coconut 124
2. The Eggs from the Hat 127
3. The Fade-Away Glass 130
4. The Imaginary Keg 133
5. Fish from the Air 136
6. Houdini's Giant Bowl Mystery 138
7. The Great Sack Escape 140
8. Canary and Light Bulb 144
9. Fish Globe Production 145
10. Aquarium Production 148
11. Duck or Rabbit Production Box 149
12. The Flying Cage 153
13. The Pop-Through Frame 154

CHAPTER 7. MENTALISM 155
1. Message Reading 159
2. Single Messages 161
3. The Untouched Card 164
4. Duplicated Thought 166
5. Color Clairvoyance 168
6. Out of the Phone Book 170
7. The Marked Name 173
8. The Random Mind 177
9. In the Crystal 180
10. Calling All Cards 181
11. Nailed Thoughts 183
12. Nine Out of Nine 185
13. Relayed Thought 188
14. The Mental Challenge 191

CHAPTER 8. GRAND ILLUSIONS 195
1. Film-to-Life 202
2. The Girl of Iron 205
3. The Drop-Away Cabinet 208
4. The Escape from Sing-Sing 211

5.	Spiked Alive	214
6.	The Glass Sheet Mystery	217
7.	Crushing a Girl	219
8.	The Cane Cabinet	222
9.	Catching a Bullet	224

ILLUSTRATIONS

Dimes and Pennies	5
Card and Glass	9
Match in Mid-Air	12
Three-Coin Twizzler	14
The Twizzle Card	17
One-Hand Knot	19
Catch the Sugar	24
The Penetrable Card	69
The Red Ribbon Pack	79
Disecto	82
The Patriotic Liquids	85
Under Cover	106
The Spirit Post	111
The Hand of Cagliostro	116
The Knotty Spook	121
The Flowing Coconut	126
The Eggs from the Hat	129
The Fade-Away Glass	132
The Imaginary Keg	135
The Great Sack Escape	143
Fish Globe Production	147
Duck or Rabbit Production Box	152
Single Messages	163
The Marked Name	176
Relayed Thought	190
The Girl of Iron	207
Drop-Away Cabinet	210
Spiked Alive	216
Crushing a Girl	221

US/Canada Magic Shops Listing 231

Foreword

A s long as there is Magic, Walter B. Gibson will remain a part of it. He was a prolific writer of books and magazines about magic. From historic books on Harry Houdini to the best teaching books on magic, Walter could write it all. He was the ghost-writer behind Houdini, Howard Thurston, Harry Blackstone, and Joseph Duninger, to name but a few. No other author has contributed as much to magic as Gibson.

No one loved writing more than Walter. In his lifetime he wrote over three hundred novels and fifteen hundred publications, although not all of them were in his name. He used "Maxwell Grant" for his very famous radio series, "The Shadow." There is not a library of consequence that will not have some of his novels and magic books on hand.

Over the years, Walter invented many top-selling magic tricks and most of them are still being sold today. Some of his popular ones are "Nickels to Dimes", "The Double Bill Tube", and "Oil and Water".

He certainly served as an inspiration to thousands of professional magicians and countless amateurs who learned magic from Walter's books. From 1927, when he wrote "The World's Best Book on Magic," to 1981 when he wrote

"Walter Gibson's Big Book on Magic for All Ages," he managed to pass his keen magical knowledge to others. He also has been the source for inventors who have used his books and magazines as a source for their tricks.

To learn magic you must start with a good teaching book, and Walter's *Mastering Magic* is the best you could find! This is a general book on magic that teaches how to perform tricks, gives some insight into the lives of the master magicians and provides ideas on showmanship. It also provides you the secrets behind many other magic tricks and big stage illusions of past and present. Although this book was written years ago, many of the elements of magic have not changed. The principles are as current today as when they were first written. In this printing, the original ideas are expanded and brought up to date. New illustrations have been added to make it easier for you to learn the tricks.

In addition, the top 23 tricks are noted with a trophy. If you can successfully perform these tricks, you will have become a "Master Magician" and will have earned the right to complete and display your diploma, found on page 229.

The tricks are distinguished with one of five icons—Easy to Perform: rabbit out of hat; Do-It-Yourself: playing card, X-acto knife and glue; Dealer Item: magic store; Historical Trick: classic magician dressed in tails; and Master Magician trophy.

A list of U.S. and Canada magic dealers—including names, addresses and phone numbers—are made available following Chapter 8. You can call or write to them for a free catalog or visit those in your hometown.

With the use of this book you will be amazing your friends and relatives with ease, as you go from trick to trick, showing off your new-found skill. You will be rewarded with smiles, applause and friendships.

When I was in my teens, I read my first Gibson book. The years have passed and now I'm over 50. My profession is inventing magic tricks, marketing, lecturing, and performing them. It has taken me all over the world. Magic is a universal language. Even when I was unable to utter a word of the language in the country I was visiting, I was still able to communicate and entertain with magic. Since magic is so visual no words were necessary.

I still use some tricks that I learned when I read my first Walter Gibson book. I am sure you, too, will find tricks from this master that you will be performing for many years.

Just as Walter wrote in "The Shadow," "The week of crime bears bitter fruit"; he could have written "the rewards of magic bears the sweetest fruit."

MICHAEL SHELLEY
MAGICAL MYSTERIES

Preface

Lifetime Books, Inc. is proud to present Walter B. Gibson's MASTERING MAGIC.

Gibson, a magician of forty years and a prolific author of magic, game and hobby books, created this classic for beginning practitioners of the illusionary art of magic.

This has been one of our bestselling books because every generation is curious in wanting to know how the master magicians perform their unbelievable tricks. With practice, you too will perform like Harry Houdini!

Featured are over 100 tricks and 30 full-page illustrations, as well as a complete list of all major magic dealers in the United States and Canada.

We hope you enjoy our latest presentation in a series of magic and hobby books. Friends and family members will be amazed as you learn how to perform like a real pro!

We do want to caution that all tricks should be practiced and carefully performed under adult supervision. Please feel free to seek advice from a professional magician or a magic store. Never use substitute items in place of the materials suggested and always use caution when handling chemicals, matches or other similar materials. Lastly, we do not advocate, promote or encourage performance of the final trick, "Catching a Bullet."

Good luck and happy reading,

Donald L. Lessne
Publisher

Biography

Walter B. Gibson, fondly known as the "Magician's Magician," learned magic by practicing with the all-time greats. Over a 35-year period, he performed side-by-side with the famous HARRY HOUDINI, HOWARD THURSTON and HARRY BLACKSTONE!

Mr. Gibson served as President of the Philadelphia Assembly of the Society of American Magicians and held the title of First Vice President of the Magician's Guild of America.

Gibson was a prolific writer. His specialties included magic, hobbies, psychic phenomena, games and puzzles. He created radio's most famous thriller: THE SHADOW, writing scripts for over 2500 episodes and nearly 300 novels (under the pen-name Maxwell Grant) based on the character.

When not performing, the legendary magician enjoyed residing in his 22-room "haunted-house" in Eddyville, New York.

Biography

This magic classic is updated and revised by magician Mike Shelley. Dozens of illustrations have been added to compliment the easy-to-understand text. Contained are magic tricks for the beginner, from teens to adult. You will learn magic by applying the strategies employed by the greatest performers.

Mr. Shelley has been performing magic for over 40 years and has been involved in all phases of magic.

He is the President of the Florida Magician's Association, President of American Magician's Assembly (#76) and is a past president of both the International Brother of Magicians Ring (#150) and of S.A.M. (#49 & #100).

As an author, he has written a column for *Magic Manuscript* and has been published in Harry Lorayne's *Apocalypse*. Mr. Shelley is the editor of the Florida State Magician's Association newsletter.

As the owner of MAGICAL MYSTERIES, he has invented and patented over 150 tricks in Mentalism, Close-Up Magic, Platform and Stage Magic. His tricks are marketed all over the world. One of his tricks, "Spots Before Your Eyes," is based on a trick contained in this book.

As a lecturer, he has spoken at the Magic Castle and at magic conventions and associations across the United States, Europe and the Middle East.

Icons

Easy

Historical

Do-It-Yourself

Dealer Item

Master

Close-Up Magic

In all forms of magical entertainment, the proper presentation of a trick or mystery strikes the keynote. All skill or cleverness will be wasted unless an effect is demonstrated properly. Yet, unless the beginner couples his practice with actual experience, he can never test his work. That is why an old adage has persisted: "The best way to learn magic is to begin doing it."

There is something in that saying but it must not be interpreted too literally. It depends a great deal upon the choice of tricks used in the early stages. The beginner must convey the impression that he is somewhat clever; that his tricks are the result of study or practice. At the same time he cannot afford the risk of disclosing subtle magical methods through his own inexperience.

Hence it is wise to begin with tricks that puzzle rather than mystify, dealing in stunts more than magic. Anything that intrigues an audience is good entertainment. If it baffles, so much the better, and if the idea itself is ingenious, people will still appreciate it if they do catch on. At that, the budding wizard holds an advantage if he carries enough arrows for his bow. By following one baffling stunt with another, he can cause the onlookers to lose the thread of things and often to forget something which they thought they knew.

This chapter is therefore dedicated to such devices—a whole collection of them. With the tricks given here, there is no worry. Simply study them, rehearse them and tell the tale. The results will speak for themselves. The experience gained from audience reactions will be invaluable when working the more secret methods disclosed in later chapters.

Admittedly, some of this close-up magic is derived from puzzles, but falls distinctly in the magical category. One great dividing line between a puzzle and a trick is that the secret of a puzzle lies in the answer and must therefore be revealed; whereas the secret of a trick need never be explained. In other terms, a trick is demonstrable whereas a puzzle is only explanatory. Close-up magic used to be called "Twizzlers." The term "Twizzler" has been coined to represent a puzzle or paradox which can be demonstrated. Seeing it accomplished, people will still have to guess the how or wherefore. That gives the Twizzler the status of a trick, which in turn introduces the element of Magic.

All these Twizzlers are intended for impromptu performance, which is the accepted way of testing one's magical aptitudes. Common objects are used and while various suggestions are made, the individual performer does not have to limit himself to those described. The basic facts thus established, the next step is to introduce the Twizzlers.

1. Coin and Saucer

This one is a "give-away," but it presents such a seemingly impossible problem that it will always command interest.

The performer opens proceedings by dropping a coin into a saucer, then pouring the contents of a half-filled glass of water into the saucer, so the coin is submerged. The trick is to remove the coin from the saucer without getting the fingers wet. No one is allowed to touch the saucer. To make it all the harder, the water must remain in the saucer after the coin is removed.

The method is quite ingenious. Light a small quantity of paper and drop it, burning, into the glass. As the paper finishes burning, invert the glass on the saucer, not over the coin but alongside it. Hold the inverted glass slightly tilted and the water will surge up into the glass. Let the glass rest upside down in the saucer, the glass Detaining the water. The coin may then be picked up without wetting the fingers.

As soon as the coin is removed from the saucer the glass is lifted and the water escapes down into the saucer again.

Younger children should not try this effect without adult supervision.

2. Dimes and Pennies

Mark a sheet of paper with seven squares or stopping places set in a row, thus:

x x x x x x x x x x

Put three dimes on the squares at the left; three pennies on the squares at the right. The middle square is vacant. The trick, or twizzler, is to transpose the positions of the dimes and pennies by a series of single moves and jumps.

Dimes can only move or jump to the right. Pennies can only move or jump to the left. The coins must be moved or jumped singly. Each move is limited to a single square. Each jump can be made only over one other coin, no more. However, it is permissible to jump a dime over a dime, or a penny over a penny, as well as jumping one coin over another of the differing type.

People may find this transportation stunt very difficult, particularly as there will only be one vacant square in which to move or jump a coin.

Here is the system: Move a dime. Jump a penny. Move a penny. Jump a dime. Jump a dime. Move a dime. Jump a penny. Jump a penny. Jump a penny. Move a dime. Jump a dime. Jump a dime. Move a penny. Jump a penny. Move a dime.

This system is very easy to remember, since it runs: one dime, two pennies, three dimes, three pennies, three dimes, two pennies, one dime. One, two, three, with a middle three, then down again, three, two, one. Where either a move or a jump is possible, the move takes precedence.

CENT CENT CENT ⟶ DIME DIME DIME

CENT CENT CENT ↶DIME ⟍ DIME DIME

CENT CENT ⟵ DIME CENT DIME DIME

CENT ⟋CENT⟶DIME CENT DIME DIME

CENT DIME CENT ⟋CENT⟶DIME DIME

CENT DIME CENT DIME CENT ⟶ DIME

CENT DIME CENT DIME CENT↶DIME ⟍

CENT DIME CENT↶DIME ⟍ DIME CENT

CENT↶DIME ⟍ DIME CENT DIME CENT

⟶ DIME CENT DIME CENT DIME CENT

DIME ⟋CENT⟶DIME CENT DIME CENT

DIME DIME CENT ⟋CENT⟶DIME CENT

DIME DIME CENT DIME CENT ⟵ CENT

DIME DIME CENT↶DIME ⟍ CENT CENT

DIME DIME ⟶ DIME CENT CENT CENT

DIME DIME DIME   CENT CENT CENT

*THERE ARE 15 MOVES IN ALL, STARTING
HERE FROM THE BOTTOM, GOING UP.*

DIMES ARE MOVED RIGHT - CENTS MOVE LEFT

THIS IS A JUMP ⟿
THIS IS A MOVE ⟶

Dimes and Pennies

3. Power of Thought

Have a person hold a penny in one hand and a nickel in the other, without telling which is which. Then state:

"I want you to multiply the coin in your left hand by two. You have it? Good. Now multiply the coin in your right hand by thirteen...Have you got it?" After the person nods, you tell him which hand holds the penny and which hand has the nickel, yet at no time has he declared the results of his multiplications.

Though this is chiefly a "catch" it will often leave people baffled. The cue is the speed with which the person responds to the final question "Have you got it?" Only a brief pause should be made before springing that question. If the victim is holding the penny in his right hand, his multiplication of one times thirteen is almost instantaneous and he nods with it. But if the right hand holds the nickel, he will hesitate before he nods. This tells you which coin is in the right hand.

A more subtle version can be worked with a dime and a nickel. In this case, have the person multiply the left hand coin by five, the right-hand coin by seventeen. He'll get the dime total quickly by simply adding a zero as the multiple of ten, but will hesitate if he is multiplying 5 by 17.

4. Drop the Match-Box

· MASTER ·

This is a tantalizing stunt that will often cause people to remain baffled without knowing why. Taking a box of safety matches, you hold it several inches above the table and drop it end downward. The box lands and remains standing on the table.

After a few such demonstrations, you invite others to try it, all dropping the box from the same height. They find that the box invariably bounces and falls over. Apparently, you alone have the knack of dropping the box just right.

There's more to it than just the knack. In holding the box upright, take it at the top end, between the tips of the thumb and fingers. In so doing, use the other hand to push the drawer open, sliding it behind the screening fingers of the upper hand.

When the box is dropped it has a tendency to bounce when it strikes. But the drawer, sliding downward and shut from the impact, provides the needed stability to keep the box upright. It shuts so suddenly that no one realizes it was open when you dropped it.

Be sure to have the box fairly well filled with matches to give it weight. The drawer should be a loose one that will clamp shut rapidly. It is also wise to experiment beforehand to ascertain the maximum height from which you can drop the box and have it remain upright. The longer the drop, the more effective the trick and the less chance of some one else accidentally causing the box to stand.

5. Card and Glass

Balancing a plastic drinking glass (just in case you drop it) on the top edge of a playing card appears to be very difficult. Nevertheless, it can be learned with very brief practice, provided you know the trick that goes with it.

Hold the card upright, thumb at one side, fingers at the other, with the exception of the forefinger, which stays behind the card. Using the other hand to set the glass on the edge of the card, raise the hidden forefinger so that it serves as a prop. The plastic glass should be set so that its center is slightly to the rear of the card, making it all the easier.

The lighter the plastic glass, the better. After a few trials, the balance can be done in convincing style, but it is most effective to make it look like a delicate, difficult job.

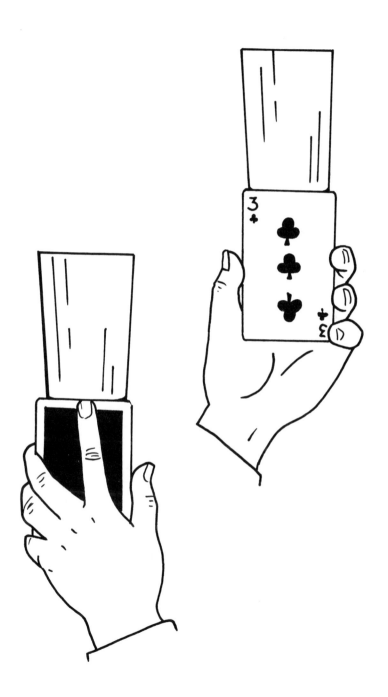

Card and Glass

6. Glass and Cigarette

A plastic glass is placed on the palm of the hand, which is held level. The fingers are tilted upward at an angle of about forty-five degrees and a cigarette is placed upon them, pointing the same as the fingers.

Now, with an expert flip, the performer causes the glass to turn a somersault, catching it as it comes upright again. At the same time, the cigarette scales higher; as it drops, the performer catches it in the glass, completing a very skillful feat of jugglery.

Actually some skill and practice are necessary, but the trick is not very difficult. The proper system is to practice with the glass alone until it can be handled deftly. Then add the cigarette, paying particular attention to placing it at the proper angle so it will go almost straight up when the glass is somersaulted in the usual fashion.

Then it is only necessary to watch the glass until it concludes its turn. The cigarette, being lighter, travels higher, and there is sufficient time to look for it after the glass has landed in the right position. By using this system, the catching of the cigarette becomes a fairly easy matter.

This trick can also be performed using a plastic glass and pencil.

7. Match in Mid-Air

·MASTER·

A match is held between the tips of the thumbs and the fingers of both hands are locked in front of it. The thumbs are raised and the match mysteriously floats in mid-air behind the interlaced hands, the head of the match showing above the hands. Finally the thumbs are lowered and recapture the match between their tips. The fingers are then spread to show the hands quite empty.

In taking the match originally, hold it between the thumb and second finger of the right hand, which enables the thumb to press the match under the nail of the finger, holding it upright. As the hands are brought together, that finger is kept folded inward, so that only seven fingers—not eight—are interlocked. The second finger of the left hand fills the space where the right second finger should be.

The thumbs are raised and the bent finger moves the match back and forth, producing the floating effect behind the screening fingers. Later, the tips of the thumbs are brought together to press the sides of the match, which allows the fingers to be drawn wide. No one will notice the absence of one finger from the interlocked hands.

While the trick can be performed with a lighted match, it is inadvisable except after long practice. With an unlighted match, there is plenty of time to set it in position and the trick can be continued longer. A large wooden match is the best to use, as the head will be seen more plainly and the hands will not have to be tilted forward, hence there is no chance of anyone spying the hidden finger. You can replace the match with a pencil or wand, to avoid playing with fire.

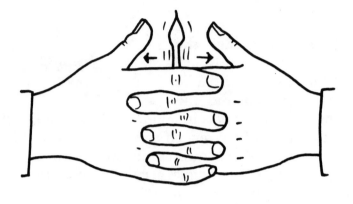

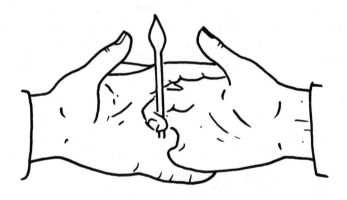

Match in Mid-Air

8. Three-Coin Twizzler

This is a very effective mystery. The performer shows three coins, preferably all quarters or half-dollars, resting upon his forefingers, which are tip to tip, the thumbs holding the coins in position from above. The thumbs should be well toward the edges of the top coin as they keep pushing that coin back and forth above the others, so that the coins are counted while in constant motion.

The coins are dropped into the left hand, which makes a throwing motion toward the right, which is also closed. Opened, the left hand shows it now has only two coins. The missing coin appears in the right band when it is opened, much to the surprise of the spectators.

This is one trick that becomes all the better, the closer it is watched. Actually there are only two coins between the tips of the thumbs and forefingers, though the performer may borrow or casually show three before he begins the trick. In any event, the third or odd coin is already concealed in the partly closed right hand before exhibiting the pair at the finger tips.

The peculiar motion of pushing the top coin back and forth with the thumbs, creates an optical illusion which makes the two coins appear as three. It must be done fairly rapidly and with a rather long motion to get the full effect, which shows best at very close range. The performer keeps mentioning "three coins" and when he is satisfied that the observers think they see that many, he drops the two in his left hand. The passage of one coin from left hand to right is then automatic, since the extra coin is already in the right hand.

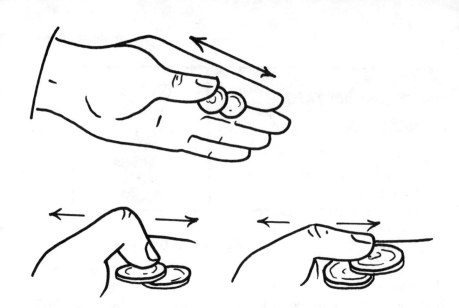

SLIDE ONE COIN OVER THE OTHER QUICKLY.

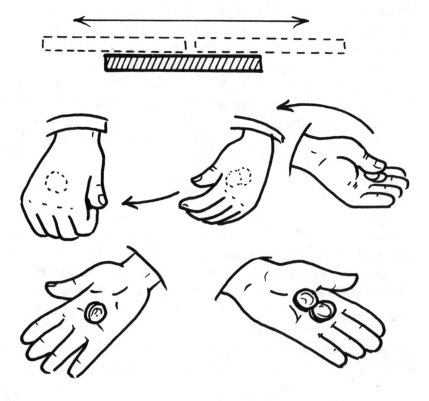

Three-Coin Twizzler

9. The Twizzle Card

One of the neatest of all twizzle tricks is the baffling card that apparently turns itself upside down or sideways when held between the thumb and fingers. It is simply a small square of cardboard, measuring about two inches each way. Across it is written or printed the word "MAGIC."

The card is held by two diagonally opposite corners between the left thumb and forefinger and the hand is slanted upward so that the word appears horizontal; that is, can be read straight across. Now the card is revolved by one of the free corners, so that it swivels between the thumb and finger. This of course is done by the right hand. On the back of the card is seen the same word "MAGIC" running straight across.

After a few such turns, the magician blows on the card and replaces it between the left thumb and forefinger. But now, when he swivels it around, the writing on the other side is upside down. Up, down, up, down, it changes with each turn of the card. Finally, the magician turns it over and the word on the other surface has gone sideways, running from top to bottom of the card. He hands the card for inspection in this condition, leaving everyone much puzzled.

The card is prepared thus: Across one surface, write the word "MAGIC." Turn the card over diagonally to the left and write the word "MAGIC" across the other side. It is then ready for operation.

In displaying the card, hold it so the word runs straight across in normal fashion, but press it between the lower left corner and the upper right. The card is thus upright, but is held catercornered by the left hand: thumb at lower left, forefinger at upper right. Now the right thumb gives the card a half revolution forward, by pressing down on the upper left corner. The result is that the word on the other side will also run straight across. This is so natural that nobody suspects anything unusual. The card may be turned over repeatedly, and every one takes it that the words run the same way.

Take the card with the right hand, blow on it, and replace it between left thumb and forefinger. This time, however, the left thumb presses the upper left comer of the card, while the forefinger is at the lower right. That is, the angle of the left hand has been changed. Now when the right thumb revolves the card (this time from the corner at the upper right), the word on the other side will appear upside down.

TOP TOP

BOTTOM BOTTOM

FRONT BACK

Another blow, a shift of the left hand, and the original status is regained. You can keep the writing upside down on both sides if you wish, then swing the card around and make it stay right side up. For the finish, shift the card so the left thumb holds it at one edge, the forefinger at the other; namely, so the hand too runs across. Then, when the card is turned over from the top edge, the two words are at right angles to each other.

When people are allowed to inspect the card, they will then be more baffled than ever.

Practice in front of a mirror and watch as you perform it. Movements must be crisp and clean in order to fool people.

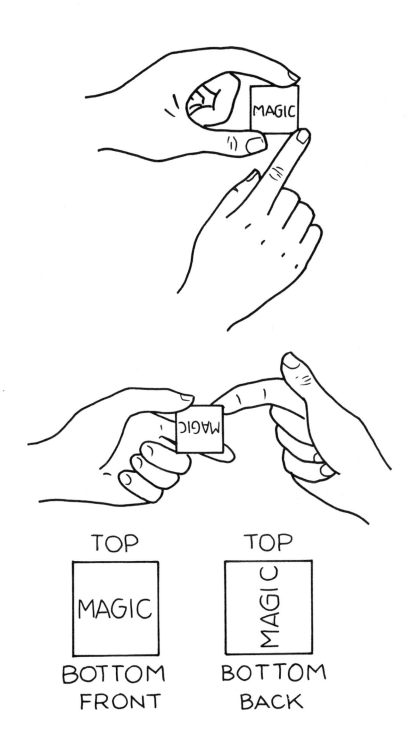

TOP

TOP

MAGIC

MAGIC

BOTTOM
FRONT

BOTTOM
BACK

Twizzle Card

10. One-Hand Knot

· MASTER ·

An adroit bit of jugglery with a handkerchief is the tying of a one-hand knot. This looks difficult but is actually very easy if a large handkerchief is used.

Hold the right hand upright, thumb pointing upward, and drape a diagonally twisted handkerchief across it. The front corner of the handkerchief should be toward the fingers; the rear corner toward the wrist. The rear corner should also hang lower than the front.

The thumb presses the front portion of the handkerchief to hold it in place. The hand then turns over, downward and inward, to the front, until the first and second fingers can clip the rear corner of the handkerchief between them. This is why a large handkerchief is needed as it helps keep the corner dangling within reach.

With the fingers and thumb pointing downward, gently shake the handkerchief over and off the hand, retaining only the corner clipped by the first two fingers. A knotted handkerchief results.

One-Hand Knot

11. Coin and Bottle

A coin is placed on a table; a soda bottle is inverted and balanced upon the coin. The trick is to remove the bottle from the coin without touching either of the two objects. The bottle must be kept in its present upside-down position.

This sounds close to impossible, but the stunt is actually quite easy, though it must be done neatly. Punch the table lightly and repeatedly with downward strokes of the fist. The bottle will jiggle itself over the edge of the coin and on to the table, still maintaining its balance.

Some practice is needed to work the stunt effectively. The bottle must not be jarred too heavily as it jiggles from the coin edge. Keeping it in slow but constant motion is the best process.

12. The Puzzling Label

This is more of a novelty than a trick; but it usually proves itself quite a puzzler. Picking up a bottle from among, some empties, you apparently discover something very curious about it: namely, that this bottle has its label on the inside instead of the outside. How that could have come about is something of a mystery.

The bottle is fixed beforehand and planted along with the others to be picked out at an appropriate time. First, a label is soaked from a bottle, then rolled about a pencil. The bottle it partly filled with water and laid on its side. The label is slid from the pencil and pushed into the bottle where it unrolls as it floats on the water.

Gradually shake the water from the bottle, letting the label settle toward the lower side, where it is easily guided to the required position. The label attaches itself to the inside of the bottle, remaining there for later display.

13. Catch-the-Sugar

This is one of those feats that "can't be done" until you proceed to do it. The required articles are two lumps of sugar and a small drinking glass or cup that can almost be encircled by the thumb and fingers.

Have someone gird his hand about the glass and hold ,a lump of sugar between the tips of the thumb and finger. The second lump is then set on the first. The trick is to flip the upper lump into the glass, then do the same with the lower, so that both lumps are in the glass.

The first lump proves easy. A mere toss and it can be caught in the glass. But every time the remaining lump is tossed, the first one flies out of the glass. That's why everyone thinks it is impossible.

Here's how you do it. Instead of tossing the second lump, hold the hand high, release the lump and drop the hand down with it. By sweeping the hand a little faster, you can bring the glass beneath the falling lump before it reaches the floor and thus catch it in the glass along with the first lump.

It takes some knack, as too rapid a swing may cause the first lump to leave the glass, but once acquired it is worth the trouble as it proves a very neat trick.

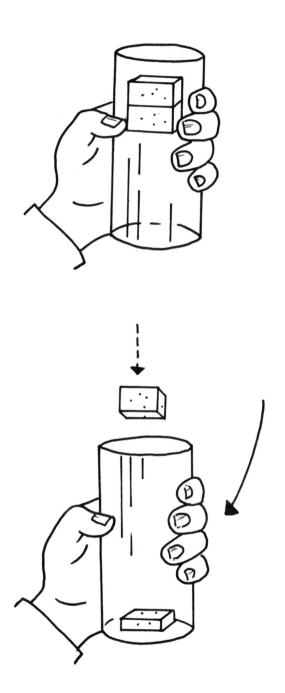

Catch-the-Sugar

2

Pocket Magic

There was a time when professional magicians confined nearly all their legerdemain to the stage, and amateur wizards were wont to copy their example. But as more and more persons took up the art as a hobby, it became the custom to perform magic on call. Any one performing magic for his friends could hardly beg off because he had no equipment handy, so there came a demand for pocket tricks, which today represent the most thriving branch of the business.

Pocket magic has been given the professional touch by Blackstone, whose skill at performing amazing close-up mysteries has set the pace for other magicians. Years ago, Herrmann used to perform odd feats of wizardry at the stage door or in the hotel dining room, finding that such marvels attracted people to the theater. Today, magic is often presented so informally that a performer must constantly be ready with some impromptu surprise.

Various pocket tricks can be performed with ordinary articles, so this chapter contains some items of that type, excluding those which depend on specialized skill that would demand long practice. There is a constant increase, however, in pocket tricks that are done with special appliances, some of which can be prepared or constructed fairly easily, though there are many that need precision made devices obtainable through magical dealers.

Examples of this type are found in the present chapter, and will give the reader a better insight into ways and means of this fascinating branch of wizardry.

1. The Penetrating Match

This ingenious effect must both be seen and tested to appreciate its baffling effect. The appliances consist of a fair-sized safety pin and a large match, from which the head has been broken off cleanly, so that the two ends appear identical.

The point of the pin is worked through the center of the match, care being taken not to split the wood. The match is slid along to the middle of the pin which is then clasped. Thus the match is impaled upon the loose bar of the pin; whichever way it is revolved, its progress is halted by the solid bar of the pin.

The performer holds the ends of the pin firmly between the thumb and forefinger of each hand, with the solid bar downward. With the second finger of either hand, he swivels the match downward until it is blocked by the solid bar. With the same finger, he presses the lower end of the match hard against the solid bar, at the far side. He gives a quick, inward snap with his finger, so the finger clears the end of the match.

The snap brings the match right through the bar, the wood visibly penetrating the steel. Swiveling the match around again, the performer repeats the snap with the same amazing result. In order that people can observe the penetration more clearly, the performer folds a small piece of paper and hangs it on the bar. Another snap, and the match comes through both the paper and the bar.

Properly practiced, the trick becomes amazingly effective, yet the method is extremely simple. When snapped, the match actually recoils from the pin, making a rapid revolution in a backward direction. This happens so swiftly that the eye cannot follow it. The result is an optical illusion of the match penetrating the pin.

The addition of the folded paper heightens the effect, serving as a background against which the action of the match can be better observed, yet still will carry the same illusion. Because of the reverse revolution, the ends of the match change places; this is the reason why the match head must be broken off and the ends made to appear the same.

2. Stack-the-Chips

This intriguing pocket trick is worked with a batch of poker chips or similar counters, which are embellished with large colored spots. Each chip has a spot on each side and in all cases the colors vary.

For instance, one chip has a red spot on one side, orange on the other. A second chip is labeled orange and yellow. Others are yellow and green; green and blue; blue and red.

Although each chip bears two different colors, some of the chips are duplicated, thus they form a sizable group.

The performer explains that he wants someone to stack the chips, picking any that he desires, but always placing spots of the same color together. For example: Suppose the person picks up a chip that has red on one side, orange on the other. If he holds it with the red spot up, he must then find a chip with a red spot and set its red side downward upon the first chip.

Assuming that a blue spot shows on top of this second chip, the person must pick another chip that has a blue spot, which is accordingly set upon the blue spot that already shows, making blue meet blue.

At any time the whole stack may be turned over, to use the color which appears upon the bottom of the stack. Sometimes this is necessary, as the person stacking the chips may run out of those that have a spot with the required color to continue stacking upward.

The object is to use up the entire stack of chips, totaling more than a dozen, by stacking them in this haphazard fashion. Should the person find the process blocked by any mistake or wrong calculation, he must begin again.

Once all the chips are stacked, persons are told to note the color of the spot that tops the stack; also the color of the spot on the bottom. They concentrate on those colors and after a few moments, the performer names them: for instance, Blue and Red.

There are fifteen chips in the set, three each of the following combinations: Red-Orange; Orange-Yellow; Yellow-Green; Green-Blue; Blue-Red. But in giving out the chips, the performer retains one so the person who does the stacking is only using fourteen.

The performer turns away during the stacking process. This gives him a chance to observe the colors of the spots on the chip he has retained, for example, Blue-Red. When the stack is complete and he is asked to name the top and bottom colors, he names Blue and Red. No matter how the stack has been gathered, those colors will be correct.

To repeat the trick, the performer gathers the chips, adding the one he already has. Secretly retaining another chip, he notes its colors to learn the top and bottom spots of the next stack.

This trick can easily be made by using a package of white poker chips. Put an Avery 3/4" dot on each side of the chips as described. This trick is also commercially available under the title of "Spots Before Your Eyes."

3. Three Medals

Three souvenir medals are used in this trick, each bearing a different design, but of the-same size and weight. Each has a hole near the top through which a ribbon has been strung and knotted, so that the medals dangle from the ribbons.

One of these medals is given to the magician behind his back. Thanks to his skilled sense of touch, he is able to name the design on the medal without even glimpsing it.

This divination depends on the ribbons more than on the medals. One ribbon can be drawn through the hole in the medal, knots and all. The second has an extra knot or two, so that it will tug slightly when its knots are drawn through the hole. The third is further knotted, so the knots will not go through the hole. Behind his back, the performer tests the knots, then brings them back to the top of the ribbon; meanwhile he has identified the medal. Thick cardboard disks of different colors may be punched with holes and used instead of medals.

4. The Mysterious Domino

This peculiar problem is performed with a large domino which fits exactly inside an ordinary matchbox. Two matchboxes are used in the trick. In one, the magician places the domino and closes the drawer of the box. The other box is opened and its drawer shown empty. Taking the two boxes, the magician holds the one with the domino in his left hand, the empty box in his right. The hands are wide apart, but with a magical gesture, the magician causes the domino to pass from the box in his left hand to the box in his right.

As simple as it is deceptive, this trick depends upon a few special properties. The domino is ordinary; so is one of the matchboxes. The other matchbox, however, is a special device. It has a label on the bottom as well as on the top. Furthermore, the drawer of the matchbox has a printed sheet pasted beneath the bottom, to represent the domino.

The magician places the real domino in the ordinary box and shows the other box empty. As he places the two boxes together, he turns over the trick box. Now, to remind the audience where the domino actually is, the magician pushes open the drawer of the empty box. The drawer being inverted, the spectators see the printed paper that represents the domino. Closing that box, the magician holds it in his left hand, turning over the box as he extends the hand.

Presumably the other box is empty, so the magician does not bother to open it. Holding that box in his right hand, he commands the domino to pass. When the boxes are opened, the one on the left is empty, while the domino drops from the box on the right.

Don't let your audience get too close for this one or the secret will be revealed. It is too easily seen by a keen-eyed spectator.

5. Jumping Rubber Band

The jumping rubber band is a very easy and popular trick to perform. Magician David Copperfield uses this trick on occasion because it is so strong.

This is literally one of the snappiest of impromptu tricks. The magician places a rubber band over the first and second fingers of his left hand, drawing it down to the base of the fingers. The band is of such size that it is slightly loose. With his right thumb and fingers, the magician snaps the band slightly to show that it is nicely in place on the left fingers.

Turning over the left hand, so that it is palm down, the magician doubles that hand into a loose fist. On the back of the first and second fingers, the rubber band is shown exactly as before. Suddenly, as the magician extends his fingers, the hand jumps from the first and second to the third and fourth.

Rather amazing this, particularly when the magician shows both sides of the left hand. Again, he forms a fist, shows the band on the back of the third and fourth fingers. As suddenly as before, the rubber band does a jump back to its original position around the first two fingers.

The tricky work begins when the magician is snapping the rubber band with the right hand. To do this, the right thumb and fingers draw the band inward from the base of the left hand fingers, the band encircling the first and second fingers. A few draws and snaps by the right hand; then, as the right hand draws the band inward as if for a final snap, the left hand is turned palm downward, doubling its fingers.

This allows all the fingers of the left hand to double themselves inside the rubber band. The result: Viewed from above, the band seems to gird the base of the first and second fingers only. From beneath, however, the tips of all four fingers are within the loop of the band.

Now, if the fingers are extended suddenly, the band will jump. Actually, it slides off the first pair of fingers and onto the second pair in a half rotary motion. To make it jump back, the right hand does not have to manipulate the band. Instead, as the left is turned palm down, the left thumb inserts itself in the loop and stretches the band across the hand, enabling all the finger tips to enter it. The tip of the left thumb immediately slides itself free and all is set for another jump of the rubber band, the moment the fingers are extended.

Practice with a rubber band will make all this clear and once the performer finds himself proficient in this snappy little trick, he can introduce another element that adds to the mystery.

The added element is this: After placing the band around the first two fingers of the left hand, the performer takes a larger band and laces it over all his fingers between the first two knuckles. That is, he loops the big band over the first finger, crosses its strands, loops it around the second finger, and so on. With this large band in place, it would seem impossible to make the smaller band jump from the base of one pair of fingers to the other.

Nevertheless, the trick works just the same. Experiment will show that the large band does not interfere with the process at all. This makes the trick look quite impossible.

6. Bottle and Pills

This baffler has the elements of an escape mystery, reduced to pocket proportions. The performer introduces a pill bottle of cylindrical shape and a few pellets which he terms pills. These pills are of a sort that will not dissolve in water as the performer demonstrates by dropping them in the bottle, filling it with water and then corking it.

Now, placing the bottle under a handkerchief, the performer produces a very puzzling result. After manipulating it a few moments, he brings out the bottle in one hand, the pills in the other. The bottle is still corked and filled with water, which raises the query: How could it be done? People who want to try it are baffled before they begin. They just can't take the pills from the bottle without pouring out the water first. Nevertheless, the impromptu wizard did it!

Here's how: The pills are actually metal pellets, painted white. Instead of pills, sequins or beads may be used, but in any case they must be metal, and of a magnetic type. The wizard also uses a tiny but powerful magnet. With his hands beneath the handkerchief, which he keeps draped over them, the magician uncorks the bottle, places the magnet at the outside near the bottom and moves it up to the top.

Magnetized through the glass, the pills come along. Once they are out of the top of the bottle the cork is replaced. The magnet can be attached to a finger ring, but in this particular trick it is better to have it concealed in the cork. It should be in the top half of the cork, so as not to attract the pills while they are first exhibited in the bottle. When the cork is removed from the bottle under the handkerchief, it is used as the magnet, then replaced.

Instead of placing the magnet inside a cork it would be easier to simply glue a magnet inside the top of a pill bottle. After affixing the magnet to the top of the cover of the pill bottle, paint the magnet to match the cover.

Though it's a great trick, it is tough to get magnets into a cork. Using a concealed magnet in the hand works best. Remember, don't let the audience get too close.

7. Self-Opening Match-Box

A quick, effective pocket trick. Somebody wants a match, so the magician extends a box of matches and invites the person to take one. As the person reaches for the box, it suddenly opens and a few of the matches fly out into his hand.

Take a rubber band and gird it around the sides and ends of the matchbox cover, lengthwise. Then push the drawer into the box, forcing in the rubber band like an inside loop. The rear of the box must be pressed firmly at top and bottom, between the thumb and forefinger, to hold the drawer.

Simply release the pressure at the right moment and the rubber band will shoot the drawer open so forcibly that some of the matches will fly out. With a light rubber band, the drawer will stop before it is clear of the box, so the magician simply pockets the box, then casually brings out an ordinary closed box in its place.

If a heavier band is used, the drawer will shoot clear and spill its matches on the table. In that case, there is plenty of opportunity to slip the rubber band from the cover and drop it unnoticed to the floor. The best box to use in the trick is a wooden safety-match box.

8. Self-Closing Match-Box

Here the magician extends a box of matches to a spectator, inviting him to take a match, since the box is open. As the person reaches for a match, the box shuts of its own accord. Much surprised, the magician pushes open the drawer again; offers a match to someone else. The provoking matchbox promptly snaps shut as it did before.

A rubber band is the motivating force. It should be a thin band, dark in color, so that it is scarcely noticeable around the sides and ends of the box, where it is placed. When the drawer is pushed open, the rubber band stretches and is all the less likely to be seen. However, the matchbox should be kept constantly in motion during the course of the trick.

Encircle the box with the band and have it ready in the pocket. Push the drawer open and hold it open by pressing the top and bottom of the box at the back, between thumb and forefinger. Release the pressure and the box will shut. Push the drawer open and the trick is ready for a repeat. A wooden box of safety matches is the type to use.

This makes a good trick in combination with the "Self-Opening Match-Box." Two boxes can be shown, one in each hand. The box in the left hand is open; that in the right is closed. A wavy motion of the boxes toward each other and the box on the left goes shut, while the right-hand box opens at the same instant.

Some practice is needed to accomplish this effectively, as the boxes must be set before the trick, each hand helping the other to make ready.

9. Magnetized Glasses

Using a book about the size of this volume, also a pair of small, light drinking glasses, the magician proceeds to demonstrate a feat of actual Oriental wizardry. This trick was originally used as a close-up mystery by wonder workers in the Far East.

A handkerchief is wrapped around the book and the magician inverts the glasses upon it, side by side, a space of about an inch between them. Pressing his first two fingers between the glasses, he slides his thumb under the book, then turns it over, handkerchief and glasses with it. Amazingly, the glasses remain suspended from what is now the bottom of the book.

Afterward, glasses and book are given for examination, to show that they could not have been attached in any manner, though the presence of the intervening handkerchief was in itself a proof that trickery was absent.

Actually, the trick is in the handkerchief, the only item that seems completely free of suspicion. Two round beads are tied together with less than an inch of cord between them. The hem of a handkerchief is opened and the beads are put inside it. In wrapping the prepared handkerchief around the book, the magician can feel the beads and ar-range them so that they are side by side, fairly near the edge of the book.

The glasses are inverted side by side, each so its rim is over a bead. As they are slid apart, the rims engage the hidden beads. The fingers are pressed between to exert outward pressure, thus holding the glasses in place when the book is turned upside down.

10. The Passing Pennies

Simple items are used in this close-up effect: some pennies and a pair of match-packs. Placing one match-pack on his left hand, the magician uses the other pack to cover a coin which is lying on the table. He lifts the pack from his hand and the penny has arrived there. Lifting the pack on the table, the magician shows that the coin has gone from beneath it.

Immediately, the magician repeats the trick, causing all the coins to travel one by one from beneath a pack on the table to his hand.

The pennies are of a special type, the steel pennies which were briefly in circulation. They are therefore magnetic and in each match-pack is a flat magnet of strong enough power to pick up such coins. Showing some pennies at the outset, the magician steals one from the group with a magnetic match-pack and places that pack on his left hand. With his right hand, he spreads the coins, picks up the other pack and sets it over a coin on the table.

Commanding the coin to pass, the magician draws away the pack from his hand, his fingers retaining the hidden penny. Lifting the pack from the table the magician shows that its coin is gone. He drops that pack over the coin in his left hand, thus adding another coin to the hand. Then the magician uses the first pack to vanish another coin from the table. Proceeding with this alternating system, he causes all the coins to travel from table to hand.

Some of the steel pennies have been copper-plated and are therefore ideal for this trick, as their magnetic quality is not suspected.

11. Three Divining Rods

Showing three small wooden cylinders, each about two inches in length and the thickness of a pencil, the magician states that they are divining rods. Each is painted a different color, as red, green, and blue. Their peculiarity, according to the magician, is that their colors can be distinguished even when they are out of sight.

To prove this, the magician supplies a metal tube with a cap that fits over it. There is a small hole in the bottom of the tube, so that when one of the wooden divining rods is inserted, the air will emerge when the rod is pushed down, as it is a fairly tight fit. The ends of all the rods are painted black, so that it would be impossible to tell them apart by looking through the hole.

While the magician's back is turned a rod is placed in the tube and the tube covered with the cap. Then it is dropped in the magician's hand behind his back. The other two rods are kept from sight while the magician concentrates on the color of the rod in the tube and soon names it correctly.

The tube, is returned to the spectators, rod and all, and the trick may then be repeated.

The hole in the tube is more important than supposed. The rods have corresponding holes in both ends, but they are scarcely noticeable, as they are smaller and painted black. Behind his back, the magician takes a pin which is fastened under his coat and presses it up through the hole in the tube into the rod.

The depth to which the pin goes tells the color, as the holes in the rod are drilled accordingly. Just past the pin point indicates the red rod. About half the pin's length means green. If the pin goes nearly all the way, the rod in the tube is blue.

12. The Rattle Bars

This is the streamlined equivalent of the famous old "Shell Game" in which the customer is always out-guessed. The "Rattle Bars" have one advantage over the older games; they are practically self-working. They are also guaranteed to exasperate the calmest mind.

The weapons in this Battle of Guess are three little bars or cylinders about an inch and a half long by a half inch in diameter. Two of them are solid, but the third is hollow and inside it is a little weight which shakes back and forth between the ornamental tips of the bar; hence the third can be heard to rattle. Otherwise the three bars are identical.

Laying the three bars on the table, the magician finds the rattler, shakes it so that all can hear, then moves the bars about. Someone is asked to pick out the bar with the loose shaker, which seems easy enough. But always, the customer picks up the wrong bar. The rattler turns out to be in another spot and the performer shakes it, then repeats the trick.

The secret lies in an extra solid bar. The performer holds this concealed in his hand. In gathering up the three bars from the table, he substitutes the extra solid one for the shaker. Laying three solid bars in a row, the magician shakes one, along with the rattle bar concealed in his hand. Hearing the rattle, people believe the solid bar is the shaker and pick that one, only to find themselves wrong.

This one will fool even the most knowledgable magician or layman.

Card Tricks

C ard tricks form by far the largest branch of magic and their performance may almost be classed as an art in itself. Formerly, the majority of such tricks depended upon skill and it was necessary to acquire certain sleights or manipulations in order to build up a repertoire. True, there were tricks that utilized mathematical systems or special setups, but these were too trivial to interest capable performers.

Today, all that has changed. Sleights still hold a place, but with card table magic supplanting that of the platform, new and more baffling systems have been devised in the field of card wizardry. First came shortcuts, eliminating the more difficult sleights; now even those are unnecessary in the presentation of a card routine. Ingenious systems, subtly camouflaged, offer a wealth of workable material.

The term "self-working" has been applied to card tricks of this sort, but should not be taken too literally. It means that such tricks will work themselves if handled or delivered properly, but they should be studied and then rehearsed before performance. The tricks in this chapter are the sort now current in the "self-working" class and those given here are largely of the dealing type, because those are most satisfactory to the impromptu card worker. Usually, card tricks are introduced at the card table. If not, a table is needed for effective close-up tricks with cards.

In learning card tricks, it is always best to do so with a pack in hand, working out each stage of the trick from the description.

1. Guess Again

This is a fast-moving trick with A surprise finish that can be learned at the first trial, but should be rehearsed until it can be shown smoothly. Any hesitation may spoil the effect.

Taking a shuffled pack of cards, the magician cuts it into two heaps by lifting the top half of the pack and placing it farther away from him, treat is, beyond the lower half as the cards rest on the table.

The performer now asks people to guess the name of the card on the far heap. Whatever they say proves wrong, so the magician turns the card up, showing it to be, for example, the Three of Spades. Now, lifting the top of the near heap, the magician glances at it, without showing it and says,

"This card would have told me that the card on the other heap was the Three of Spades. You don't believe it? I'll prove it for you."

He completes the cut, so the pack is entire again. He then cuts off about half and places it as the far heap. Looking at the card on the near heap, he states, "The card on top of the other heap is the Nine of Clubs." The card is turned up and sure enough, the magician is correct. He completes the cut, squares the pack, makes two heaps again. Looking at the card that tops the near heap, he says that the top card of the far heap is the Ace of Diamonds. Showing that card, the magician proves he is right again. He goes right on with the trick, repeating it as often as he wishes.

The method is absurdly simple. The opening spiel is merely an excuse for the magician to glance at the top card of the near heap. When he completes the cut, by placing the near heap on the far, and then cuts the pack again, the card that topped the near heap becomes the top card of the far heap.

Already knowing that card, the magician has only to name it (say the Nine of Clubs) but first he glances at the top card of what is now the near heap. This puzzles the spectators, making them think that it has some bearing on the trick, and they don't stop to realize that the magician already knows the top card of the far heap.

Meanwhile, under their very noses, the magician is learning a fresh card (say the Ace of Diamonds) which becomes the top card of the far heap on his next try. That is, the magician is really working "one ahead" and simple though the operation is, it proves more and more baffling with each repetition, as the spectators are trying to figure it out on the basis of a mistaken theory.

What clinches the trick is the climax. As described so far, the trick could go on indefinitely and would therefore wear itself out. To avoid this, the magician suddenly states that he actually doesn't have to look at one card to name another. Without looking at the top card of the near heap, he says, "Here we have the Five of Diamonds." Picking up that card, he reaches for the top card of the far heap, adding: "And this is the Ten of Spades." Picking up that card too, he drops both face up on the table and they prove to be the cards he named.

Actually, the Five of Diamonds is the card on the far heap. Knowing it, the magician calls it as the top card of the near heap. Picking up the card that tops the near heap, he sees it to be the Ten of Spades. So he promptly reaches for the card on the far heap saying, "And this is the Ten of Spades." Plucking the far heap card, with his right hand, he places it with the card from the near heap, which he is holding toward him in his left hand. He then drops the two cards face up, showing that both his calls were correct.

This neat climax was introduced by Ted Annemann, who specialized in adding unusual twists to tested tricks. Not only is it the perfect finish; it also serves to dim any glimmers in the minds of sharp spectators regarding the simple factor involved in the earlier stages of the trick.

2. Find Your Own

This is a card trick with a participation feature that nonplusses all concerned. Apparently it is done entirely by the spectator, which makes it highly effective when done in group fashion, as will be detailed later.

Telling a spectator to take ten cards, the magician asks him to remember any card and its position from the top of the packet, for instance, the Five of Spades, three cards down. Neither the card nor the number is mentioned to the performer, however. Taking the packet, the magician looks through it, returns it to the spectator, saying he has already learned it.

To prove this, the magician tells the person to move the number that he noted, card by card, from the top of the face down packet to the bottom. If the spectator had noted the third card, he would transfer three cards singly from top to bottom.

Without having watched the transfer, the magician then tells the spectator to move a card from top to bottom and deal the next card on the table. He is to move another from top to bottom, again deal the next card, and so on—move, deal, move, deal—until he is holding just one card. When the spectator looks at that card, it proves to be the one he originally noted, in this case the Five of Spades.

The trick is automatic, but with one detail that people do not observe and which therefore makes the trick an easy deception. In pretending to find the selected card, while glancing through the packet, the magician transfers five cards—half the packet—from the bottom to the top; that is, from the front of the packet to the back. From then on, the trick works itself, regardless of the spectator's number. In being told to transfer his own number from top to bottom, he is simply counting more or less, as the case may be, and the chosen card will always be at the position required for the final deal.

As a group trick, this has been elaborated by the famous Blackstone, for use with an impromptu audience. As many as five people are given ten cards each. If more packs are available, they may be distributed so that a dozen or more spectators are participating at once. The magician glances at each packet in turn, after a person has chosen a number and noted the card at its position. Of course with each packet, the magician cuts half the cards from bottom to top.

All the participants transfer their respective numbers top to bottom, go through the dealing process, and each finds himself holding his selected card. This multiplies the surprise and heightens the mystery proportionately.

3. As Many As You

Though absurdly simple in execution, this trick proves utterly perplexing to those who witness it. Only after it has been tried can its results be fully appreciated. Then it will stand constant repetition, particularly when the performer completes it with the climax that will be described.

Handing a pack of cards to a spectator, the magician tells him to remove a batch of cards, not more than about fifteen. This done, the spectator returns the pack to the magician who takes off a batch of his own. Counting his cards, the magician states,

"I have as many as you, four more, and enough to make you twenty-one."

The magician then asks the spectator to count his cards and name the total. Suppose the person says he has twelve cards. From his own batch, the magician counts off twelve—the spectator's number—and then counts off four more, laying them aside. Here be pauses, saying, "Remember, I said I have enough more to make you twenty-one." Then:

Counting his remaining cards: "Thirteen, fourteen, fifteen—," and so on, the magician finishes triumphantly with the last card on the count of "Twenty-one!"

Shuffling the pack again, the magician lets the spectator remove a batch. Taking some of his own, the magician counts them and says, "I have as many as you, five more, and enough to make you nineteen." Suppose the spectator has eight. The magician counts off eight from his own batch, lays aside five more, then counts his remaining cards: "Nine, ten, eleven—", and so on, ending with precisely nineteen.

From reading this description, it may sound surprising that the magician's count should always end exactly on the number. When doing the trick with cards, dealing them as explained, the surprise is much greater. The more people try to figure it out, the more it puzzles them, because they are looking for complications where there are none.

All the magician has to do is make sure that he takes a larger batch of cards than the spectator. That's the reason for suggesting that the spectator remove a number of cards under fifteen." At that, the magician should have no trouble taking more even should the spectator go a few cards over his quota. If the pack looks as though too many have been taken the performer simply removes a larger bunch than usual.

In counting his own cards, the magician doesn't worry about how many the spectator took. That will take care of itself when the time arrives. The magician simply counts a small number like four—which is to serve as a throw-off—and then counts his remaining cards, which we shall suppose total twenty-one. The magician then says to the spectator: "I have as many as you, four more, and enough to make you twenty-one."

Of course the magician has as many as the spectator and enough to make him twenty-one, because all the magician does is count to the spectator's number when he learns it; then continue counting from there to twenty-one. For example, if the spectator has twelve cards, the magician counts up to twelve, then later resumes his count on thirteen. If the spectator had only had five cards the magician would have counted off five, then later resumed the counting with six, and so on up to twenty-one. In between, however, the magician pauses to deal off the "four more" before resuming the count. It is the emphasis on those extra cards-which mean nothing, that makes the whole thing a perplexity.

Repeating the trick generally bewilders the witnesses all the more, but sometimes there are skeptics who begin trying to crack the whole thing down. For their benefit, the magician can introduce the following convincer. Assume that the magician has just ended one demonstration with a count of nineteen. He has all the cards replaced on the pack, adding his nineteen last of all. In so doing, he notes the bottom card of that packet—say the Six of Hearts—which is therefore nineteen from the top.

The magician invites the spectator to take off a batch of less than fifteen cards. That done, the magician removes a group. Suppose the spectator took eight. This time, in counting his cards, the magician notes the faces. He finds the Six of Hearts eleven down in his batch. Subtracting eleven from nineteen, he knows that the skeptic has eight cards.

This time, the magician reverses his statement. Suppose in counting his cards he finds he has twenty-one. He then says, "I have eleven cards, three more, and exactly your number left. Don't tell me your number until we come to it."

The magician then counts off eleven from his group. He next counts three more in another group. Holding the rest, he says, "Now let's count our cards together." Dealing card for card, the magician and the skeptic find that they each have precisely eight, which proves that the magician did strike the correct number. This adds a bona fide touch to all the previous demonstrations.

4. The Double Clock

Taking a pack, the magician deals two circles of cards face down. There are twelve cards in each circle, hence each is termed a "clock" but there is no need to regard any of the cards as representing numbers on the dial.

The magician simply asks one spectator to run his hand around the clock on the left, stop on any card and pick it up with the two cards next to it. He is to look at those three cards and count the total of their spots. If any face cards are among them, they are to be counted eleven, twelve, thirteen, for Jack, Queen, King respectively.

Suppose that the person finds his three cards to be a Three, a Five, and a Ten. This gives him a total of eighteen, a number which he is to remember.

Someone else does the same thing with the second clock, picking three cards in a group. He is asked if the trio contains a face card. When he says "Yes," the performer tells him to remember its suit, then add the value of the other two cards to gain a number. Thus, assuming the person picks up a Jack of Hearts, a Seven of Spades and a Two of Clubs, he is to remember Hearts and also Nine, the total of seven and two.

Giving the balance of the pack to a third person, the magician tells him to count down to the number indicated by the three cards from the first clock. In this case, that would mean a count down to the eighteenth card. That card is then compared with the finding from the second clock, which represented Nine and Hearts. To the surprise of all, the eighteen card proves to be the Nine of Hearts!

The pack is arranged for this trick beforehand. The top twelve cards are in the following rotation, regardless of their suits: Five, Ten, Three, Five, Ten, Three, Five, Ten, Three, Five, Ten, Three. When these cards are dealt in the form of a clock dial, it doesn't matter from what spot a person picks out three cards that are together. Those three are bound to be a Three, a Five, and a Ten, whatever their order. Thus their total will surely be eighteen.

Under those twelve cards is another setup which runs as follows: Ace of Hearts, Seven, Two, King of Hearts, Seven, Two, Queen of Hearts, Seven, Two, Jack of Hearts, Seven, Two. The suits of the spot cards do not matter; they may be in any rotation. When three cards are taken from this face-down clock, all in a group, there is bound to be a face card which has Hearts for its suit. Also, the two accompanying cards are sure to total nine. Thus the trio represents the Nine of Hearts.

Eighteen cards further down in the pack, at position forty-two (since the two clocks require twenty-four cards) the magician has planted the Nine of Hearts. Thus the spectator who deals from the remainder of the pack will find the indicated card at the designated position.

Before dealing the clocks, the magician may run through the faces of the pack letting the audience see them, as no one will notice the setups. After cards have been drawn from the clocks, the leftovers from both circles should be gathered together. Still face down, thus obliterating, their arrangement.

Other combinations may be used for the circles, but the performer should always be sure to specify an Ace counts as a face card, in case one is drawn from the second clock.

5. Three-Deal Prediction

· MASTER ·

Taking a shuffled pack of cards, the magician looks through the faces and states he will predict a card that a spectator will subconsciously select. The magician writes the name of the card on a slip of paper which is folded and placed aside for future reference.

Spreading, the pack face down along the table, or running the cards from hand to hand, the magician tells the spectator to take three cards absolutely at random. Giving the pack to the spectator, the magician then instructs him to lay the three cards face up, side by side, and upon each card deal enough more to bring its total up to ten. The magician mentions that an Ace counts one, while any face cards stand for ten.

As example: Suppose the three cards are an Ace, a Seven, and a King. Upon the face-up Ace, the spectator deals nine cards from the pack; upon the Seven he deals three; upon the King, none.

That done, the spectator is told to add the values of the three cards he took. In the case mentioned, the Ace, Seven and King would count for one, seven and ten respectively, producing a total of eighteen. The spectator is told to count that many down in the pack and look at the final card—in this instance the eighteenth.

Suppose that card is the Four of Spades. When the spectator opens the folded paper, he finds the name "Four of Spades" written on it!

This trick works almost automatically. After a pack has been shuffled, the magician takes it and runs through the faces of the pack, secretly counting until he reaches twenty, from the face or bottom of the pack. This card, which will be the thirty-third from the top, is the one he predicts.

When the pack is spread face down, the magician merely sees to it that the three cards which the spectator takes are all above the thirty-third. This is easily handled by not spreading the bottom portion of the pack. Now, no matter what three cards the person takes, his deal and the count that follows Will bring him out on the thirty-third card.

Suppose the person takes three Aces. In dealing, he must bring their total up to ten, meaning thirty cards in all. Then he counts the values of the cards originally dealt: three Aces, totaling three. He counts that many from the pack and looks at the final card, which is therefore thirty-three. If higher cards than Aces are dealt, the count in each case is correspondingly less. The count simply subtracts from the deal.

Make sure beforehand that a complete pack is used and that it contains no joker. If there is a joker, you must count twenty-one cards from the bottom to make the prediction, instead of twenty. Should the spectator take a card below the thirty-third when the pack is spread, take a deep one yourself, lay it face up and explain how you wish him to count. Then put that card back in the deck, nearer the top. Another system to avoid trouble is to give the person half the pack and let him take three cards from it, while you look through the other half to make a prediction. Replace his half on top of yours and proceed with the trick.

6. Color Sense

As a dealing trick, this forms a pattern from which a variety of effects have been developed. In the direct form given here, it would seem that the performer was able to distinguish red cards from black while a spectator is dealing them, face down.

The performer tells a spectator to shuffle a pack; then begin dealing cards, face down. After a while, the performer tells the spectator to stop dealing and retain the balance of the pack. Picking up the dealt cards, the performer says: "You dealt just four more reds than you now have blacks in your hand. We'll count them and see." Running through the dealt heap, face up, the magician weeds out the red cards and counts them, finding sixteen. The spectator goes through the cards he holds, face up and discovers to his surprise that he has just twelve black cards.

The system is simply this: Take a pack of cards and divide it into two equal heaps of twenty-six each. Spread the heaps face up and you will find that you have exactly as many black cards in one heap as red cards in the other. If one heap has fifteen blacks, the other will have fifteen reds. Conversely the first heap will have eleven reds and the second heap eleven blacks. Though this sounds puzzling, it is simply a natural fact. The numbers may vary, but heaps will always balance in terms of reds in one heap, blacks in the other.

The trick of "Color Sense" is merely an extension of that fact applied to unbalanced heaps. Move a card from one equal heap to the other, making the heaps twenty-seven and twenty-five respectively. You will then find one more black in the larger heap than there are reds in the smaller heap. There will also be one more red in the larger heap than there are blacks in the smaller. For each card moved to the larger heap, the ratio will increase by one card more.

All the magician does when the spectator deals is keep counting the cards. As the count nears twenty-six, the magician says for the spectator to deal several more cards and then stop. Suppose the spectator stops on thirty. Being four more than twenty-six, four will be the ratio. Picking up the larger heap, the performer asks the spectator's preference: red or black. If red is stated, the performer says: "You dealt four more reds than you have blacks." Should the spectator pick black, the performer words it: "You dealt me four more blacks than you have reds." Either way, the fact is proven when the heaps are weeded.

The trick can be done with less than a full pack, provided an even number of cards is used. For instance with thirty-four cards, the magician must remember that seventeen is the balance point and handle things accordingly. In this case, should the spectator deal twenty cards, he would be giving the performer three more blacks than reds; also three more reds than blacks.

This trick may be repeated, but it is more effective to follow it with other dealing systems given in this chapter.

7. Faces Up

Taking a pack of cards, the magician turns a batch face up and riffles them in among the others so that the pack becomes a mixture of face-up and face-down cards. The magician invites a spectator to shuffle the pack thoroughly so there will be no chance of guessing which cards are which way.

Receiving the much mixed pack from the spectator, the magician places it behind his back, if he is standing, or beneath the table if he is seated. He says that without looking at the cards, he will tell which are face up and which are face down.

Shortly, the magician brings out the pack in two heaps, one in each hand. He states that be has divided them so that each heap contains exactly the same number of face-up cards. The heaps are spread by two spectators; each weeds out the face-up cards. They come to exactly the same number—say eleven face-up cards in each heap.

The trick is based on the rule of "balanced" heaps. Half of the pack (twenty-six cards) is turned face up, at the start, though the exact number should never be mentioned. No matter how thoroughly shuffled the pack may be, the performer has only to put it out of sight and count off the top twenty-six cards.

The situation will then be this: Either heap will contain exactly as many face-up cards as the other heap has face-down. That is, if the right-hand heap has eleven cards face up, there will be eleven face down in the left-hand heap. But this trick doesn't stop there. It has an added feature.

Having separated the two heaps, the performer turns over the cards in his left hand, while it is still out of sight. By doing this with the left-hand heap, he literally transforms its face-down cards into face-ups. Then when he brings the heaps into sight and gives each to a different person, a count of the cards will prove that each heap contains the very same number of cards face up!

It is a good plan to do this trick with less than a full pack, though not too many less; for example, from about thirty-four to forty-two, always using an even number. There are two reasons: Not only is the secret deal more rapid, but the spectators are not anxious to guess the number of cards that were originally face up. That number is generally different after the trick than at the start and with a full pack, someone might suspect all was equal at the outset.

Too few cards are also likely to betray the secret, hence the value of using an even total in the high thirties or low forties. There is also a neat throw-off that can be used with a considerable quantity of cards. Before receiving the pack, the performer asks that it be cut until there are some face-down cards on top. Taking the pack, he slides these over slightly and notices how many there are, say the three top cards.

The pack out of sight, the performer counts off the top half and Rips over the lower half, in the left hand. Then from the right-hand group, he pushes the three top (face-down) cards onto the left. Thus though the face-ups are equal in each heap, the heaps themselves will prove unequal should anyone decide to count them afterward. This will puzzle people who think they have a clue to the riddle.

8. Sure-Win Poker Hand

Taking ten cards, the magician lets a spectator shuffle them and deal two hands of five cards each. When the hands are turned up and studied for poker combinations, the magician has the winning hand. This is repeated with the same ten cards, which either the magician or spectator may deal after the shuffle, and always the magician's hand wins.

The method is easy, but the magician must "sell" the trick by his presentation. Use three groups of three alike, such as three Kings, three Queens, three Jacks. The tenth card is an odd one. By seeing to it that the odd card goes into the spectator's hand, the magician is sure to win.

If the pack is of "one way" design, with an ornamental back that looks different from the others when the card is turned around, simply have the odd card turned opposite to the rest. With a symmetrical pack, bend a corner of the odd card or nick the edge slightly, enough so it can be spotted.

After the spectator shuffles the cards, take them and fan them slightly, saying "Just ten cards." This enables you to note whether the extra card is an odd number from the top or an even number. If an odd number, deal the hands yourself; if even, let the spectator deal. Should the spectator prefer to deal, tell him, "Remember, you have just ten cards which you shuffled yourself." Then count them, one to ten, before handing them to him. But in counting, draw off one card with the right thumb, draw off the next so it falls upon the card first drawn, and continue thus. The result: The extra card, if originally at an odd number, will now be at an even number, so the spectator will get it when he deals the hands.

Another process is to let two hands be dealt, watch where the indifferent card falls, and simply pick up the other hand. With a borrowed pack, this is very satisfactory as nobody can claim that the pack may be marked. In any case it is good to work the trick with one spectator after another, rather than with only one person. This gives an excuse for spreading or counting the cards after each shuffle, as you are explaining to each new individual the general idea of two poker hands.

The combinations work out thus: If the spectator gets a pair (such as two Kings) you will beat him with two pairs. Should he get two pairs, you will beat him with three of a kind. If a spectator picks up three of a kind, your hand will have three of a kind and a pair, thus winning with a full house.

9. The Identical Cards

This is one of the most effective of two-pack tricks, because it is suited to continued repetition. The magician and a spectator each shuffles a pack of cards. Looking through his pack, the magician draws out a card and holds it face down. From his pack, however, the spectator selects a card without looking at it. Each person inserts his card in the other's pack, face down. The magician cuts his pack, the spectator does the same. Then each runs through his face-down pack until he comes to the strange card.

Each card is turned face up and they prove to be identical. For example, the magician will have a red-backed Ten of Diamonds from the spectator's pack, while the spectator will find a blue-backed Ten of Diamonds from the magician's pack.

One good trick deserves another, but this time it's so good it calls for the same. The exact process is repeated, the magician picking the card he prefers from his own pack, the spectator making a blind draw from his pack. Inserted in the other pack, the cards are found by the spread and prove identical, for example, the Nine of Spades. This continues time after time.

The method is artfully simple. Before starting the trick, the performer secretly obtains one card from the spectator's (red-back) pack and adds it to the bottom of his own (blue-back) pack. In the case cited, the card would be the Ten of Diamonds. This steal of an odd card can be done openly by holding the red-backed pack in the left hand and sliding its top card a trifle to the right with the thumb. The right hand is holding the blue-backed pack, with the hand above, fingers at the outer end, thumb at inner. In casually bringing the hands together, the thumb and fingers of the right hand pluck away the loose card from the pack in the left hand.

In shuffling his pack, the magician uses the riffle or dovetail method. He lets the bottom cards fall first, thus keeping, the odd red-backer out of sight on the bottom. In looking through the faces of his cards, he notes the card from the other pack (Ten of Diamonds) and picks the duplicate (Ten of Diamonds) from his own blue-back pack. This card goes into the spectator's pack face down. The magician, in return, receives an unknown card from the spectator's pack. This is pushed near the center of the magician's pack.

One cut of the pack accomplishes all that the magician requires. It brings the spectator's Ten of Diamonds above the unknown card. Thus, in running through his pack face down, the performer first comes to the red-backed Ten of Diamonds. He lays it on the table; the spectator does the same with the blue-backed card he received from the magician's pack. Naturally, they match, when turned face up.

To repeat: Houdini his pack with its faces toward the spectators, the magician runs through the cards remarking, "You can see I might have taken any one of these cards." In doing this, he runs across a red-backed card the strange one that the spectator actually inserted in his (the magician's) pack. The magician cuts the pack at this point, turning it face down as he carries the red-backed card to the bottom. He is then set to repeat the trick, using whatever card the strange one turns out to be, for instance, the Nine of Spaces.

Obviously, the trick can be repeated as often as desired, but it should not be overdone. The final problem is getting rid of the odd (red-backed) card at the conclusion. One way of doing this is to bring it to the bottom as before. Then, announcing that the trick is finished, the magician picks up the spectator's pack with his left hand and drops his own pack on top of it. He then either lays both packs aside, or, needing one pack for another trick, spreads the two packs near the division, and thus separates them where the blue-backs end and the red-backs begin. In either case, he has added the odd card to the pack in which it belongs.

Another system is for the magician to announce, without bringing the odd red-backer to the bottom of the blue-back pack, that he can place some of his cards in the spectator's pack and whatever cards the spectator may call for, he will find them among the cards that the magician inserted. To demonstrate this, the magician simply takes both packs and riffles them together. He hands the double pack to the spectator while squaring it together and says: "Name any of my cards you want. You'll find them there." This makes a laughable finish and also disposes of the odd card, as it will simply appear to be another red-backer when the two packs are sorted.

10. Nine-Card Deal

Nine cards are dealt face upward on the table in an overlapping row. Tapping them with his finger, the magician counts them in order from one to nine. He asks a spectator to pick any number and remember the card at that position. Gathering the nine cards, the magician replaces them in the pack. He asks the spectator to name the number at which the mentally selected card was placed, but not the name of the card itself. As soon as the number is stated, the magician reveals the card in a surprising fashion.

The climax of this trick is apt to vary, hence the only way to cover the full effect is through the explanation. In dealing the cards, make sure that the one which arrives at number five position is a card whose value can be spelled with exactly three letters, such as an Ace, a Two, a Six, or a Ten. If such a card does not land at number five, shuffle the cards and deal again or simply rearrange them.

After a person has mentally selected a number between one and nine, also remembering the card at that position, you gather the nine cards. Next you turn away and take the card at the fifth position (which might be the Ten of Diamonds) and turn it face up in the group. Put the batch on the pack and give it a cut, to place the nine potential cards in the middle.

Then state, "I have divined the card that was selected and have placed it where it will reveal itself as soon as you state its number in the row. Do not tell me the name of the card; just give the number of its position and I shall prove that I knew it all along."

If the chooser states that the card was at position five, simply spread the pack and there it is, face up, proving your claim. If any other number is announced: "I have turned one card face up and it is the card that will indicate the exact position of yours."

Should the person give position four, you spread to the face-up card and remove it with the card just above it. Turn the two over and show that the face-up card is face to face with the one selected. For position three, spread to the face-up card and say: "Note that this card is a Ten. I shall spell the letters in its name and thus come upon your card."

Beginning with the Ten of Diamonds, you spell upward, touching card by card: "T-E-N." Turn up the final card. It is the chosen one. For position two, do the same process, but start spelling with the card just above the Ten of Diamonds. For position one, start spelling with the card above the Ten, but turn up the next card after you complete the spelling.

Number six is treated like position one, except that in turning the two cards over, the chosen one is revealed back to back with the Ten of Diamonds. For seven, spell the same as for two, but downward toward the bottom of the pack. For eight, spell downward as with position two. For nine, spell downward as for position one.

Such spellings as A-C-E, T-W-0, or S-I-X are simply the equivalents of T-E-N, so the trick will work if any card of those values should happen to be the key at number five.

4

Platform Magic

T
he exigencies of present-day magic have been met
by the development of many tricks which can be
carried in small space, set up rapidly, and presented under almost any circumstances. Most of these are
tricks requiring special apparatus of the sort to be described.

Formerly, small apparatus was used chiefly in platform
shows, wherein the magician had something of the benefit
of a stage, insofar as arranging his setting and allowing for
angles of vision were concerned. Now, the magician may
be called upon to perform at a banquet table or in the center of a nightclub floor, which means that he must meet
problems for which much of the old-style apparatus was
not designed.

Furthermore, many magicians now specialize in short
acts, often giving more than one performance in an evening. They must get their tricks ready promptly and pack
them up rapidly after finishing the act. Hence a suitcase
show is adaptable to a variety of conditions and constitutes
the stock-in-trade of many progressive performers.

It is possible to classify such tricks in a large number of
divisions. In the catalogs of most dealers they are listed

under such titles as "Bottle Tricks," "Comedy Magic," "Flower Magic," "Liquid Tricks," and other descriptive headings. These of course are the impression that the audience gains of the tricks in question, but this book is dealing with magic from the performer's standpoint, hence the grouping is general.

1. The Quick-Change Handkerchief

The magician displays an ornamental handkerchief of red silk surrounded by a white border. His left hand forms an upright fist; over it he drapes the handkerchief with his right hand so that the silk is directly atop his left fist.

The right forefinger pokes the center of the handkerchief down into the left fist. Dipping beneath, the right thumb and fingers grip the silk and whip it through the left fist. Most amazingly, the handkerchief has changed from red to green and it is promptly spread between the hands to show that the transformation is complete. The handkerchief is laid aside and the hands shown thoroughly empty.

Sheer simplicity makes this trick effective; that, plus convincing procedure. The handkerchief is red on one side, green on the other; however, this cannot be noticed because of the white border, which is the same on both sides. In first displaying, the silk, the magician holds it so that only the red side shows; then he drapes it on his left fist and pulls it through.

This pull-through reverses the handkerchief, showing the green side instead of the red. But as the right hand completes the pull, the left thumb and fingers grip the corners of the handkerchief. The right hand comes up promptly and takes the front, or top corner, at the right. The left hand retains the top (or front) corner at the left. The handkerchief can then be spread, showing the green side only.

Done quickly and cleanly, the whole procedure is so natural that spectators will avow they saw both sides of the handkerchief before and after the change.

2. The Wandering Milk

The magician begins this one by filling a small glass with milk and placing the glass in an empty hat. To prove that the hat is empty, he removes the glass of milk, shows the hat empty and puts the glass back into it.

Picking up a few sheets of paper, the magician rolls them together to form a tube, which he girds with a rubber band. Having more sheets of paper handy, he rolls them and puts them inside the tube already formed. Taking the glass of milk from the hat, the magician covers it with the paper cylinder that he has formed. To make the cylinder still stronger, he rolls an extra sheet of paper and slides it down inside the cylinder, between the cylinder and the glass.

All is now ready for the vanish. A few magic passes and the magician tosses the tube in the air. It falls lightly to his hand—nothing but an empty paper tube, which he shows to the audience so that everyone can see right through it. Then, reaching into the hat, the magician brings out the glass of milk.

A special appliance is required for this mystery. It consists of a cylinder made of transparent celluloid, slightly larger than the glass that is to be used. The celluloid cylinder is painted white, almost to the top, the white paint representing milk. This "fake" as it is termed, is placed in the hat beforehand.

First the magician fills the ordinary glass with milk but makes sure its level is not quite as high as that of the painted fake. Putting the glass inside the hat, he sets it in the fake.

Remembering that he has not shown the hat empty, he brings out glass and fake as one. After showing the hat empty, he puts glass and fake back in the hat.

Forming a tube of papers and girding it with a rubber band, the magician adds a few papers inside the tube, where they expand to the full size of the improvised cylinder. Now reaching in the hat, he brings out the fake alone. Setting it on his left hand, the magician covers the fake with the cylinder, the fake passing for the actual glass of milk. Finding an odd sheet of paper, the magician rolls it and states that he will insert it in the cylinder between the cylinder and the glass. Actually he rolls it tightly enough so that it goes inside and through the fake which the spectators think is the glass. There, the final sheet of paper expands.

When the tube is tossed and shown empty, people see nothing of the fake because it is now encircled, inside and outside, by sheets of paper held firmly by the rubber band. The fake having no bottom, people see right through the cylinder and the effect is excellent, because everyone is thinking of a solid glass with the added weight of a full load of milk. People immediately wonder where the glass could have gone and when the magician brings the original glass of milk from the hat, the mystery is complete.

3. The Penetrable Card

As an experiment in passing one solid object through another, the magician introduces a giant playing card, measuring about four times the dimension of an ordinary card. Also the magician has a wooden frame, just large enough to receive the card. This looks like a picture frame except that it is of heavier construction. In addition, the frame is fitted with a broad wooden band or crosspiece which runs horizontally across the center.

Inserting the playing card in the frame, the magician shows it front and back, then sets the frame upon a stand, or easel, which has a large base and a skeleton frame attached. The purpose of the skeleton frame is to support the wooden frame that contains the giant playing card. The two frames are about the same size, in terms of outside measurement.

In the center of the crossbar attached to the wooden frame there is a round hole filled with a circle of leather, cut in slits, line the spokes of a wheel. Thus, though the card can be seen above the crossbar and below, its center is obscured, but obviously must be directly behind the hole in the crossbar.

Taking a pencil, the magician pushes it through the center hole. Next he pokes a handkerchief through, then a wand, and finally his finger. Plainly, the center of the giant card must be punctured. But such is not the case. When the magician removes the card from the frame, he shows it to be undamaged and may even pass it for examination.

All this depends upon a rather ingenious arrangement, which mostly concerns the frame. Purposely made over the frame. Purposely made oversize, the frame has a greater width than the space between its top section and the cross-bar, which in turn is equal in width to the frame. In the top of the frame is a segment of a playing card, giant size of course, of just the size to fill the space between the frame top and the crossbar.

Similarly, the crossbar hides another segment of a play-ing card, designed to fill the other gap. When the frame is inverted, these segments slide down from their biding places and give the appearance of the giant card itself.

The frame is of double thickness, with a space between. There is an opening at one end, originally the top, but at the other end, the entire frame is solid. When the magi-cian drops the giant card down through the upper slot, it stops, squarely placed in the frame. When he turns the frame around to show the back of the card, he inverts it, but holds the giant card in place.

This causes the two slides to fall into place behind the openings. When the magician turns the frame around again, without inverting it, the false segments are seen, as they are arranged to fall in front of the genuine card,

The easel on which the frame is placed is hollow and has a horizontal slit cut in its top. As soon as he puts the frame on the easel, the magician releases the giant card which drops down into the easel, the top edge of the card coming below the crossbar. Any objects may then be thrust through the hole without encountering the giant card.

At the finish, the magician draws the giant card upward with his fingers until it is again centered in the frame which he then inverts, letting the card fall out while the segments slide back into their original hiding places.

This is one of the most popular-selling magic tricks and is made in plastic and sold as the Penetration Frame.

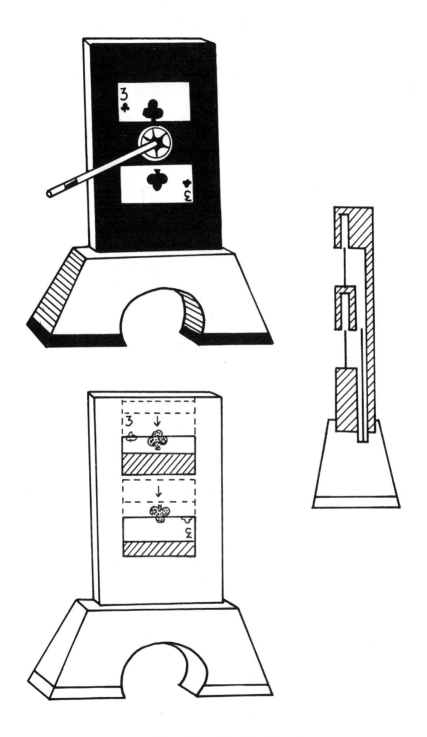

The Penetrable Card

4. Modern Vanishing Glass

The "Vanishing Glass" has long been a popular trick with practical magicians. The effect is startling and direct. A glass is filled with liquid; over the glass the magician throws a handkerchief. Carrying the glass beneath the cloth, the magician approaches the spectators, gives the handkerchief a sudden fling by one corner and the glass has utterly vanished, along with its contents.

To accomplish this, the magician uses the double handkerchief—two handkerchiefs sewn together around the four borders. Between these is a wire ring, of the same diameter as the mouth of the tumbler to be used in the trick. In covering the glass, the magician finds the wire ring, holds it through the cloth and lifts it as though it were the glass. Disposing of the tumbler meanwhile, he approaches the audience, gives the handkerchief a toss by the corner and shows that the glass has disappeared.

So much for the final effect of the vanish. An earlier problem is the disposal of the glass. Originally, the glass was dropped on a servante, or special tray behind a draped table. Later, magicians preferred to drop the glass in a black art well, cut in the table top itself and Tried with black velvet to match the table top. Various other devices have been used, but the one to be described is the most practical of all and perhaps the most ingenious.

In beginning the trick, the magician fills the glass from a large bottle. He places the glass on an undraped table, throws the handkerchief over it, lifts the glass beneath the handkerchief and at the same time sets down the bottle. Subsequently the glass disappears from beneath the handkerchief in the orthodox fashion size, painted black and bearing an appropriate label. The trick lies in the bottle.

It is a metal bottle of quart fake bottle has no bottom, but more than half way up it has a horizontal partition that serves as a false bottom. The upper half of the bottle can therefore be filled with liquid. The magician begins by pouring a glass full of liquid from the top half of the bottle. He covers the glass with the double handkerchief that conceals the wire ring. He lifts the ring, leaving the glass on the table. As he brings the handkerchief forward, with one hand, he simply sets down the bottle with the other hand, putting it right over the glass which is standing on the table behind the handkerchief.

Since the lower half of the bottle is bottomless, it fits over the glass with plenty of space to spare. From then on the magician concentrates upon vanishing the glass from beneath the handkerchief, which is easy enough, considering that the glass is no longer there.

The bottle should have a hole in the back so that the magician can insert his finger, press the glass against the inside of the bottle and lay the bottle aside, the glass going along within it.

5. The Vanishing Ink

Filling a glass with ink, the magician sets it upon a tray and exhibits an ornamental tube, just large enough to cover the glass. Showing the tube to be absolutely empty, the magician states that it has unusual magical properties. To demonstrate these, he lifts the glass of ink from the tray, sets it on his hand and covers it with the tube.

When the magician lifts the tube a moment later, the ink has entirely disappeared, yet the tube is as empty as it was originally. The magician holds it so that people can look clear through it and keep wondering where the ink went.

Now for the explanation. Inside the tube at the outset is a cylinder of celluloid, slightly larger than the glass used in the trick. This cylinder is painted black, almost to the top, but with a clear stretch above the black. Being slightly larger than the glass, the painted cylinder will go around it. However, the celluloid cylinder fits rather snugly in the ornamental tube, hence cannot be seen when inside it, particularly as the tube is painted black on the interior.

The celluloid cylinder is in the tube at the outset of the trick and the tube is standing on the tray.

The glass used in the trick is of special construction. It has a small hole drilled in the bottom. Over this hole is placed a disk of celluloid, held in place by an application of vaseline. Thus the glass can be filled with ink, without danger of leakage.

The tray is also a special one. It has a double bottom about an inch in depth, which allows a space between the bottom proper and the false bottom above. The tray is made of metal, hence the false bottom is sufficiently rigid to support the weight of the glass when the latter is filled with ink. There is a hole about an inch in diameter in the false bottom and projecting up through this is a spike or prong, affixed to the actual bottom of the tray. Painted to match the tray, the spike will not be seen, as it extends only about a quarter inch above the hole in the false bottom. Also the ornamental edges of the tray are raised sufficiently to hide this prong.

When the magician fills the glass with ink, he next exhibits the tube that contains the celluloid fake. Explaining that the tube fits neatly over the glass, he illustrates the fact by dropping the tube over the glass. In lifting the tube, the magician leaves the celluloid fake behind. There is no difference in the appearance of the glass because the celluloid fake fits neatly around it and the black paint circling the fake corresponds to the ink within the glass.

Setting the glass on the tray, the magician places it so that the spike presses up through the hole in the bottom of the glass. This raises the vaselined celluloid disk and the ink flows down into the tray. The passage of the ink is not noticed because of the black-coated celluloid fake that now encloses the glass. While the ink is flowing, the magician shows the tube quite closely to the audience, emphasizing its emptiness. He picks up the glass, squeezing the celluloid that circles it, rests the glass on one hand, picks up the tube and covers the glass.

This time, when the tube is removed the celluloid fake is taken with it. The tube can then be shown apparently empty, while the ink has obviously vanished from the glass. Tube and glass are laid upon the tray, which is put to one side.

The "Vanishing Ink" is an excellent trick when worked in combination with some other effect. One good procedure is to reproduce the milk in an empty glass. This is done with the aid of a celluloid container, slightly smaller than a glass, that has a wire loop extending above it like a handle. This is hung on the back of a draped table before beginning the trick.

Showing a handkerchief, the magician lays it on the table so that it is somewhat spread and extends over the back of the table. He exhibits an empty glass with one hand and picks up the handkerchief with the other. A finger engages the wire loop and brings the container up beneath the handkerchief. The glass is set on the table so that both hands are free to drape the handkerchief over it. During this process, the container, ink and all, is lowered into the glass.

In this trick—-as with others involving ink—special ink tablets can be used to give the water a black color. Much thinner than actual ink, such a mixture can be washed from the glass and the tray without leaving stains. Watch out for ink stains. They will undoubtedly get all over your hands.

This is a dealer item that is no longer being made.

6. Adhesive Milk

An ordinary milk bottle is shown partly filled with milk. Placing a sheet of paper over the mouth of the bottle, the magician clamps his hand upon it and inverts the bottle. He peels away the sheet of paper and the milk remains transfixed in the bottle.

The milk is real enough, for the spectators can see its new level in the bottle, now that the bottle has been inverted. The problem is: What can be holding it there? There is only one answer—Magic! To prove this, the magician takes a long, thin metal skewer and pushes it up through the mouth of the bottle. The end of the skewer appears above the level of the milk.

This process is repeated several times, and finally the milk is poured from the bottle into a pitcher. At any time, the magician can cause the remaining milk to cling within the bottle when the latter is turned upside down.

The trick is accomplished with the aid of a simple disk made of wire screen, its edge bordered with a thin strip. This disk is inserted in the neck of the bottle, being made to fit there snugly. When the bottle is inverted, the milk will not flow through the screen, because the holes are too small to admit sufficient air.

In brief, the wire fake acts exactly like the sheet of paper that the magician first placed across the mouth of the bottle and then removed.

The convincing part takes place when the magician pushes the thin skewer up into the bottle. All he needs is a skewer thinner than the holes in the screen. He can push it up and down as he pleases, simply stabbing through the openwork of the wire mesh.

When the bottle is tilted at an angle, air is admitted and the milk will flow out through the screen, but as soon as it is brought back to the vertical, the milk will stay in the bottle.

A neat way to introduce this trick is to have the bottle covered with a regular milk cap or top. The bottle is full of milk and can be opened under the noses of the spectators because the screen disk is deep in the top of the bottle proper, and therefore hidden by the milk.

Covering the bottle with the paper, the magician inverts it, holds it over a pitcher and peels away the paper. The small surplus of milk drops from the top of the bottle in very convincing style, while the rest of the milk remains. The magician then slants the bottle, pours out some of the milk, and covers the bottle with the paper again. He peels away the paper, the bottle remains half full, and the demonstration is made with the skewer, as earlier described.

The modern presentation of this trick is done with a clear plastic gimmick with a hole in it that fits over the mouth of a soda or beer bottle. It is easy to find.

7. Bottle and Rope

The bottle used in this trick resembles an Oriental jar of squatty pattern with a narrow neck. Stating that the curious bottle has magnetic properties, the magician shows a length of rope which he claims is of the very sort used by Hindu rope climbers.

Dipping the rope into the bottle neck, the magician shows that it enters quite freely. But the rule of the Hindu Rope Trick is that what goes up does not come down. Therefore, in this case, what goes in will not come out. When the magician lifts the rope by the upper child, the bottle comes up with it, clinging mysteriously to the lower end of the rope.

The bottle may be swung back and forth on the rope end. Finally, still dangling from the rope, it is lowered into the hands of a spectator. Instantly the magnetism ceases. The rope comes free and the spectator is left with the bottle, which he may examine as much as he desires.

This trick is an improvement on a "Rope and Vase" trick wherein the rope was wedged in the neck by means of a small rubber ball. That version, though effective, required some manipulation at the start and disposal of the hall at the finish, whereas this trick is automatic.

A special rope is used. It contains a thin rubber tube attached to a bulb which is hidden in the hand at the upper end. Within the rope, near the lower end, is a tiny bulb of much thinner rubber. When the magician secretly squeezes the large bulb, the tiny one inflates inside the rope and swells sufficiently to support the bottle which should be of lightweight plastic. When pressure on the large bulb is relaxed, the bottle drops free.

8. The Red Ribbon Pack

This mystery is quite a contrast to the usual form of card discoveries, as it involves a pack specially arranged to be threaded on a red ribbon. The pack does not have to consist of playing cards; in fact, those used for other types of games are preferable, since the pack is employed in this trick only.

The distinctive feature of the pack is that each card has a vertical slot cut up the center, running less than two-thirds the length of the card and measuring about a half inch in width. It is best to have these punched out by a die, so that the cards will be uniform. The purpose of this slot, which has a margin at each end, is to allow the entire sack to be strung upon a red ribbon a few feet in length.

Showing that the pack consists entirely of different cards, the magician allows one to be selected and returned. He gives the pack to be shuffled and later runs through the faces of the cards to show that the chosen one—known only to the person who drew it—is buried somewhere in the pack.

The pack is strung on the ribbon, the ends of which are held by spectators. Even then, the cards may be spread to show that the chosen one is not on the top or the bottom. With the pack hanging on the center of the ribbon, the magician covers it with a handkerchief, reaches beneath, and states that he will find the chosen card.

A few moments later, the magician draws a card face down from beneath the cloth, brings it along the ribbon and carries it from the end, which is released to allow the passage of the card. It proves, when shown, to be the chosen card.

Ribbon and pack may then be examined with special stress upon the fact that no duplicate cards are used.

The secret is quite ingenious, with a neat feature that makes the operation of the trick nearly automatic. There is no fakery whatever in the construction of the pack. It all depends on the length of the slot cut in the cards. The length of the slot is precisely the same as the actual width of each card. Moreover, the slot is not quite centered. It is punched so that it runs about a quarter-inch closer to one end of the pack than the other.

After a card has been removed, the magician turns the pack around. Thus, with the slots all set the same way beforehand, the chosen card will be reversed when it is replaced. This fact is not apparent until the pack is hanging from the ribbon, so the magician does not actually dangle it until he has covered the pack with the handkerchief or is about to do so.

Thus the chosen card will project slightly from the others, either downward or upward. Downward is preferable, so the pack may be dangled freely without the projecting card being noticed. Under the handkerchief, the magician finds this card by its projecting end. Separating the pack at that point, he points the card crosswise and thrusts it through the slotted centers of either section of the back.

In drawing the card into sight along the ribbon, it should be held in a vertical position like the rest of the pack at that point, to avoid any clue to the method whereby it apparently penetrated its companions. Stiff cards are the best for a pack of this sort, as they can be shuffled without snagging the slots.

To make this trick up yourself you can use all thirteen cards from one suit instead of a complete deck.

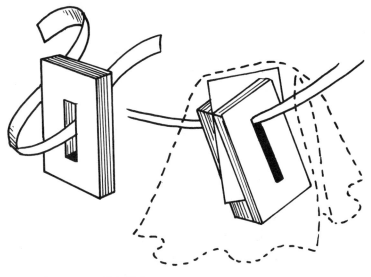

CHOSEN CARD

CUT IN DECK OF CARDS
IS 1/4 INCH CLOSER
AT ONE END.

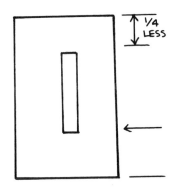

1/4 LESS

The Red Ribbon Pack

9. Disecto

The wave of "torture illusions" that came into popularity some years ago have
found their counterpart in
smaller effects, suited for the
platform. Thus, instead of chopping a girl piecemeal and
then restoring her—as will be explained in a later chapter—magicians are sometimes content to perform such
operations on a smaller or restricted scale.

It is not commonly known that these lesser effects in the
department were originally intended as preliminary demonstrations leading up to the stage illusions themselves.
Such was the case, and several excellent small effects were
designed for such purpose only to be discarded because
they took something of the interest from the larger effects
that followed.

However, out of such experimental work developed a
group of smaller torture effects that are fine for the club
and platform worker, because of their portability. In such
a category come the "choppers" or miniature guillotines,
one type of which is herewith described and explained,
under the appropriate title of "The Gay Blade."

This device consists of a block or frame, built like a thin
stand and mounted on a pedestal. The frame is made in
two sections, so that a sharp blade like a cleaver can be
slashed from top to bottom within the halves of the frame.
One end of the blade is pivoted to the frame itself; at the
other end of the blade is a handle, so that when swung
downward, the handle describes a long arc.

Midway in the double frame is a hole large enough for
the insertion of a person's wrist. A victim is selected from

the audience and watches while the magician swings the blade downward, through and past the hole. To show that the blade is really sharp, the magician puts a carrot in the hole and cuts it in half with a sweep of the blade. Then the person from the audience is invited to insert his wrist. He does so and the magician gives the blade another downward slash, right through the wrist, which is promptly removed, still on the arm and quite unharmed.

The trick is convincing because the pivoted end of the blade projects from beyond the frame. Also the portion of the blade that apparently cleaves the wrist can be seen above the frame when the blade is raised; below after it has made the chop. Yet despite this, the blade never contacts the wrist.

This is because the pivoted end of the blade is simply a dummy. It is connected with the handle by means of a large curved rod that circles up above the frame and over to the handle, apparently nothing more than a special support to keep the long blade from wavering during its down-sweep. Thus the part of the blade that sweeps through the wrist-hole is actually a short length connected to the handle.

The handle itself is long and hollow on the side away from the spectators. At the handle end of the fake blade is a knob that the magician can engage with his thumb. When he is ready to "chop" the person's wrist, he brings the handle down just far enough to hide the blade in the slit between the frames, then draws the short blade into the handle with his thumb, releasing it the instant he has chopped past the wrist, so that the full blade appears in the space below the frame.

This trick is now being made by Abotts in Colon, Michigan and by Supreme Magic in England. (This trick was called the Gay Blade.)

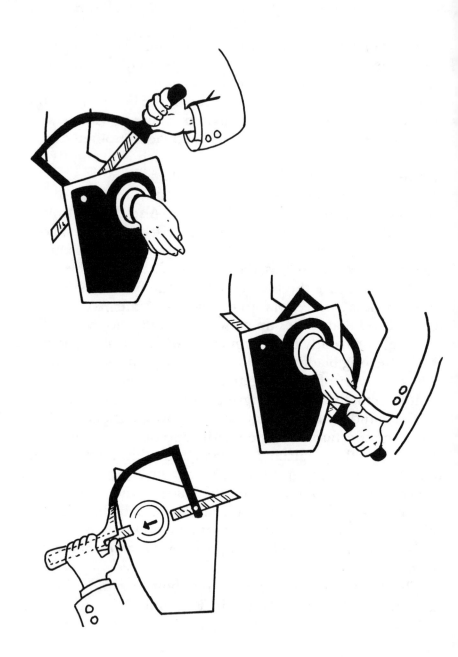

Disecto

10. The Patriotic Liquids

On a tray, the magician has a dozen small glasses containing what he terms "Patriotic Liquids." Four glasses hold a red liquid, four a colorless liquid which is used instead of white, while four are filled with a blue liquid.

Showing a tall, thin glass container of the type called a hydrometer jar, the magician next exhibits an empty tube of similar proportions. He sets the tube over the jar, then proceeds to pour the liquids into the covered jar.

First red, then the white (or colorless) and finally the blue. Glass by glass, the magician follows this rotation. He pours all the liquids slowly and carefully to insure the magical result. This is seen when the magician lifts the tube from the tall glass jar.

Instead of the liquids being a darkish mixture, they appear in perfect layers, exactly as poured, running red, white, blue, and repeating that rotation three times, from the bottom of the jar to the top.

The secret is very neat. The red and blue liquids are chemically colored. The white, or colorless, contains oxalic acid, which is a bleaching agent. When the liquids are poured into the covered jar, they all become colorless. Inside the tube, however, is a snug-fitting cylinder of celluloid, painted with horizontal stripes of red and blue with a colorless space between.

The cylinder cannot be observed inside the tube when it is casually shown empty. After the pouring, when the tube is lifted, the celluloid tube is left around the jar, which it fits rather closely. This accounts for the "layers" of liquids which the spectators observe when the tube is lifted.

Unlike most chemical effects, this trick is particularly baffling to chemists who witness it. They can understand how it could be done with liquids of different densities, but not to the extent of a dozen such. The unsuspected celluloid tube with its painted layers is the factor that makes this trick into a real mystery.

Be careful whenever dealing with chemicals. An adult should always supervise young children.

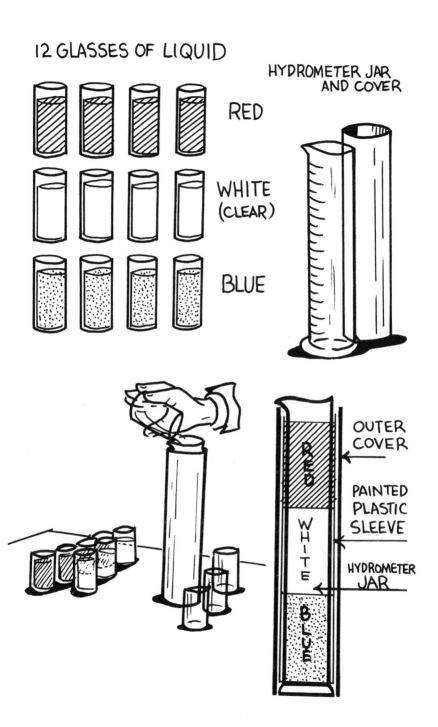

The Patriotic Liquids

11. The Penetrating Liquid

Taking a bottle of colored soda water, the magician pours its contents into a tall metal can that narrows from bottom to top and is furbished with an outward slanting rim. On this he places a sheet of glass, upon which he sets an inverted funnel.

Gripping the can with one hand, the handle of the funnel with the other, he turns them over, pressing the glass firmly between. He sets the tip of the funnel in the empty bottle, holding the glass sheet steady so that the can remains inverted upon it.

Naturally, the liquid does not escape from the can because the glass prevents it. The magician is then ready to perform a minor miracle. He commands the liquid to penetrate the glass. Instantly, the liquid begins to flow from the funnel until it fills the bottle. Lifting the can from the glass, the magician rattles a wand inside it, showing that the liquid is really gone and therefore must have penetrated the sheet of glass.

This is a clever combination of two special devices. One is called the "Foo Can" because it was first introduced by the Chinese magician, Ching Ling Foo. This can has a slanted partition running from one side of the top to the other side of the bottom, inside the can. There is a space, however, at the bottom of the partition.

When the liquid is poured into the can, the magician has only to invert the latter in the proper direction and the liquid—which only half fills the can—will go into the hidden compartment and remain there. This accounts for the can's being empty at the finish.

The funnel is also tricked. It is actually a double funnel, one within the other, the outer funnel tapering more sharply than the inner. Under the handle of the funnel is a tiny air-hole which is covered with a bit of gummed cellophane tape after the double funnel is filled with liquid, which is done beforehand.

By loosening the tape with his fingernail, the magician causes the hidden liquid to flow from the funnel into the bottle, giving the illusion that it has penetrated the sheet of glass from the can above.

12. The Vanishing Candle

The magician lights a tall candle which is standing in a candlestick. He covers the candle with a cloth that has a slitted hole in the center, so that the top of the candle and the flame are still in sight. Lifting the candle from the stick, the magician carries it forward, snuffs out the flame, and tosses the cloth in the air. In a trice, the candle has vanished and the cloth is shown completely empty.

The candle is a wooden dummy except for the top, which is a little metal cup containing the tip of a real candle. The candlestick is hollow, consisting of a tube that runs clear down inside the bottom of the base. A pin runs through two holes in the candlestick, near the upper rim, to keep the imitation candle in place.

In covering the supposed candle with the slitted cloth, the magician plucks away the tip which now has a burning flame. His other hand, steadying the candlestick, pulls out the pin and the bulk of the candle drops out of slight before the cloth is lifted. The metal cap has two tiny clips on its under side. Blowing out the flame, the magician turns back the cloth and uses the clips to grip the false tip between his fingers, so it is out of sight behind his hand.

After showing the cloth, unquestionably empty, the magician lays it aside, letting the concealed candle-tip drop within its folds.

This was the old method. The more modern method uses plastic or steel.

13. Card, Seal, and Ribbon

While essentially a card trick, this effect has the type of audience appeal that goes well with an act of varied magic, since articles other than the cards are required in its performance.

The magician hands someone a pack of cards, requesting that a card be drawn and that the person write his name across its face. The card is returned to about the center of the pack, which is turned face upward and cut. The card at which the magician cuts—say the Jack of Spades—obviously is not the selected card since it has nothing written upon it.

The magician takes a large gold seal which is attached to a ribbon. He sticks the seal on the corner of the face-up Jack of Spades, which is still resting on the pack, and has someone put his initials on the seal to verify it. With the pack still face up, the under half is cut and placed upon the Jack, thus burying, it.

Asking the person who chose the original card to name it, the magician learns its identity—say the Six of Diamonds. Giving the person the free end of the ribbon, he tells him to pull the Jack of Spades from the pack and have another look at it. The spectator does so; to his surprise, he finds that the card attached to the seal is now the Six of Diamonds, bearing his signature, and that the seal is the one with another spectator's initials.

The trick depends on a "key card," in this case the Jack of Spades. The corner of the card at the outer left has been clipped off by using a finger nail clipper. Thus by riffling the pack at that corner, the magician can always stop at the Jack of Spades, as it leaves a sharp gap when it falls.

The chosen card, when replaced, goes directly upon the Jack of Spades. At this point, the pack is face down; the cards should be the sort that have a pattern running to the edge, with no white margin, so that the missing corner of the Jack will not be noticed.

Turning the pack face up, the magician cuts to the key card by riffling the outer corner, which is now at the right. Thus the Jack of Spades is face up, with the chosen Six of Diamonds just below it. The magician keeps his thumb over the missing corner of the Jack as he holds the pack.

The gold seal is attached to the ribbon by means of a small sticker, the end of the ribbon being glued between them. This of course has been prepared beforehand. The seal itself has no gum, but the smaller sticker is so provided. Hence in moistening the seal, the magician dampens the sticker only. The seal, when placed on the corner of the pack, covers over the missing corner of the face-up Jack. The sticker, however, does not touch the Jack, but fastens itself to the card beneath.

When the pack is cut and the ribbon is pulled, the card that comes from the pack is the chosen one. While the spectators are identifying the signed card and the initialed seal, the magician scrambles to the key card, secretly removes it and drops it in his pocket. An unprepared Jack of Spades can already be in the pack in case any one asks to see the cards.

It's a really great effect. This is good for the expert or the beginner who wants to look like a pro.

14. Sands of Sahara

Showing two shallow metal pans, shaped like oversized saucers, the magician calls attention to the fact that one is filled with sand, which he states is direct from the Sahara desert. Pouring the sand back and forth from pan to pan, the performer adds that it would really take a magician to cause anything to grow in such a dry substance.

Bringing the pans mouth to mouth, the magician sets them on a small stand or pedestal. A few magic words, then the pans are lifted and spread apart, each coming mouth upward. Instead of sand each pan is filled with a blooming bouquet of colorful desert flowers.

Each pan has a circular depression in the bottom. Over one lies a metal disk painted like the interior of the pan. Attached to the under side of the disk is a bunch of expanding flowers made of paper. A similar bunch is attached to the pan itself. A pin runs through the side of the pan, holding the disk in place.

After pouring a small quantity of sand back and forth, the magician leaves the pan with the hidden flowers on the top of the pair when they are placed mouth to mouth. He pulls the pin in setting the pans on the stand and the disk drops to the lower pan, covering the sand which has sifted down to its depressed bottom.

The top pan is quickly turned upright and the flowers spring wide, filling both pans. These paper flowers are equipped with double-spreading springs, so that they can be packed compactly, yet will make a large display when opened.

Known as "Spring Flowers," they were invented by the famous magician, Buatier de Kolta, who also invented the celebrated "Vanishing Bird Cage" and a series of brilliant stage illusions. Simple though the construction of the flowers was, it didn't impress magicians until during one of de Kolta's performances some of the flowers fluttered out into the audience.

From these samples, thousands of duplicates were made and sold to magicians. Today they are listed as accessories in nearly every dealer's catalog and are purchased in lots of twenty-five or more.

This trick is now history, but the spring flowers have remained and are a part of many magicians' bag of tricks.

Mysticism

Pervading the magical scene today is the "Midnite Spook Show," with its thrills, chills, and everything else from glamour ghouls to vanishing vampires. This type of entertainment has to a great degree supplanted the lesser road shows that once played the local opera houses, but despite their emphasis on the weird, the better Ghost Shows are actually magical extravaganzas condensed to an hour's length. Spooky effects are sprinkled through the act and the windup is a "blackout" that fulfills all the qualifications of the old-time spirit seance.

This represents an interesting evolution. A century ago, there occurred the now-famous "Rochester Rappings" in a house near that city, which caused the gullible public to believe that there might be a ghost in every home. Soon a group of itinerant performers were capitalizing on the craze, most notably the Davenport Brothers, Ira and Erasmus, who presented an act that had the public guessing, not only in America but abroad.

Bound with ropes, in a four-sided opaque screened area approximately 5 feet wide by 5 feet long by 7 feet high, the Davenports caused all sorts of spooky things to happen.

Guitars strummed, bells were pitched through windows of the cabinet. Their show ended with a dark seance in which ghosts floated out over the audience. The consensus of opinion in that day was that the Davenports had genuine psychic powers, whereas actually they were skilled at getting in and out of ropes. Today, catalogs of knots and splices feature the "Davenport Knot" as a type that can be slipped or tightened as desired. Also such volumes classify a "Tom Fool's Knot" which closely resembles the "Davenport Knot" and was invented to trick the famous brothers during their tour of England.

As a boy, Harry Kellar traveled with the Davenports. Later, when he became the Great Kellar, the leading magician in America, he included a rope-tie in his program. Kellar also used Spook Cabinets in his performance and a Kellar Cabinet was a feature of the Thurston show. Blackstone became a specialist with the rope-tie and his performance of this mystery has rivaled that of Kellar. It was Blackstone, too, who introduced "Spook Nights" as special attractions with his regular show.

All this coincided with the steady enlightenment of the public in regard to magic. Its recognition as skilled artistry applied to purposes of entertainment increased the popularity of magic and diminished belief in the supernatural claims, which performers like the Davenports once intimated were theirs (even though they may not have openly avowed them). The same applies to other kinds of spookery which were constantly duplicated and eventually taken over by magicians from the purveyors of the pseudo-psychic.

Thus the midnight shows which begin with a display of streamlined magic and climax with a series of ghostly gambols are accepted by the public in the same mood with which they view the horror movies that accompany such performances. The chilling moments are interspersed with spots of comedy relief that add up to good entertainment.

Chief credit for creating this vogue goes to Neff the Magician, who toured the country billed as "Doctor Neff and his Madhouse of Mystery," reviving interest in magical entertainment along with the thrills of the Spook Show. The dramatic quality which Neff has added to the presentation of magic has rated him among the "greats" in the art.

Neff's finale consists of a medley of "dark seance" effects in which his entire company participates, thus producing a mass of ghostly manifestations. Just as stage illusions represent magical methods scaled to the size needed for the theater, so do spook shows have a direct relation to the dispirit" effects that are frequently performed in more limited surroundings.

The tricks in this chapter all belong in the spook category, from impromptu effects through those which require a darkened seance room, and up to more elaborate presentations designed for the stage. Some performers specialize entirely in such effects, but usually the spook tricks are introduced as individual features in a magical routine.

Sometimes the lesser feats are performed as byplay with the other effects. This often depends upon the size of the group witnessing the performance. The "dark room" and "cabinet" effects are the sort that once were used by pretended mediums and in some instances can be traced back to such origins. But the closely guarded secrets that once belonged to the fraudulent fraternity could scarcely compete with the modern magical methods that have been applied to the development of spook tricks.

Much has been written of Daniel Home and other celebrated mediums who flourished a few generations ago. Could they drop around today to witness a first-class job of magical spookery, they would be the most baffled members of the audience.

1. The Spirit Answer

·MASTER·

Stating the spirits are ready to answer suitable questions, the performer takes a pad of paper and inserts a sheet of carbon between the two top leaves. He asks some one to write a question on the top sheet, asking, "Are you ready to answer questions?" Under the question the person is told to sign his name.

Tearing the sheet from the pad, the performer removes the carbon paper and shows the second sheet. There is the carbon writing, but for some uncanny reason, the wording has been changed. Instead of the question, the statement appears: "This certifies that the spooks can answer questions." Underneath the statement—and this is the puzzling part—appears the carbon copy of the person's signature This is an excellent impromptu spook trick, depending on a neat device. The carbon paper is just slightly larger than the pad, to all appearances, but actually, it is about one-half longer. That extra length is folded under very carefully and creased to make it appear as the edge. That is the "edge" which is pushed up to the top of the pad, between the first two sheets.

The answer is already on the second sheet, written there through carbon paper. When the question is written on the top sheet, it is not transcribed, because two layers of carbon are face to face. But the signature, being written lower, is reproduced through the single carbon.

Several ordinary sheets of carbon paper should be handy, all cut to the approximate size of the pad. The folded carbon is picked as if at random, replaced with the others after the trick and can be slipped from the batch later.

2. The Polar Ghost

Announcing that he can at-tract ghostly visitants from the icy North, the performer asks a person to hold out his hand with the thumb straight up-ward. Raising his own hand high, the performer brings it downward and points his fingers straight at the person's palm, keeping his own thumb upward.

The person is amazed to feel a slight breeze emanate from the magician's fingers. This can be repeated with other persons, including the most skeptical, yet all will sense the uncanny touch of cool air.

This trick works automatically. Keeping his hand straight, the magician brings it down with an easy sweep, stopping with the fingers a few inches from the spectator's palm. This creates air currents which swirl from around the magician's hand and gradually reach the other person's palm, as though the performer's pointing fingers projected the cool breeze.

For a follow-up, or variant, the magician can run his hand a few inches above a spectator's outstretched forearm and a peculiar spooky breeze will accompany the action. This is done by leaning toward the person's arm and secretly breathing along it. This of course should be timed to the passing of the hand above.

3. The Talking Key

Dropping a key into a narrow drinking glass or a wide-
mouthed bottle, the per-
former calls upon the spooks
to answer questions by causing the key to strike the answers.

A system can be decided upon, such as one clink for "Yes" and two for "No." Immediately, the ghosts go to work. As he holds the glass in his outstretched hand, the key lifts itself and delivers the required strokes. The spooks can make the key count up to numbers as an additional service. The glass can be rested on the table while the clinks occur. Afterward, glass and key may be given for inspection.

A heavy glass, a lights key, and a loop of thin black thread are the only requirements. The thread is put through the hole in the key; then each end of the thread is wound around a vest button. The key may be carried handily in the vest pocket, as the loop of thread should be more than a foot in length. Experiment will determine the precise measurement most satisfactory.

The key is dropped in the glass, which is taken in one hand. This hand is advanced until the thread is taut. Then, the slightest forward motion of the hand, or withdrawal of the body, will cause the key to lift. An immediate reversal of the motion and the key will fall, accounting for clinks.

In moving from person to person as he carries the glass or sets it down, the performer finds an opportunity to make a slight turn when he is ready to conclude the trick. At this point, the free hand secretly snaps one end of the thread.

Setting the glass on a table or handing it to a spectator, the performer promptly walks away, the thread running through the hole in the key and traveling along with him.

Breaking the other end of the thread, the performer lets it fall unnoticed to the floor and no evidence remains to reveal the mystery.

Today, the black thread has been replaced by invisible thread which is so fine it can be used right before your eyes and you will not be able to detect its presence. This invisible thread is available from your favorite magic dealer.

4. The Spooky Weights

This is perhaps, the most remarkable of pretended psychic effects, well worth the experimentation and practice that are required to accomplish it.

The appliances are simple: a row of empty bottles, all with corks. Through those corks pass cords which dangle down into the bottles, each with a fish-weight on the end. Each bottle has a single cord and weight, given the appearance of a pendulum.

Gathering a group about the table, the performer places his hands upon the edge and asks every one to concentrate upon the weights. The performer is seeking to have unseen forces swing the weights—whether they are forces from another sphere or the power of thought coming from the people present.

Soon the spooky pendulums begin to sway—first one, then another. They gradually halt when required and in other ways obey the command of the performer. Yet all the while, the hanging weights are isolated from all contact.

What does it is a slight motion of the table. This is applied by the performer through pressure of his hands. By pressing and relaxing, the weights can be caused to swing and be otherwise controlled. This can become a subconscious action on the performer's part; all he has to do is keep watching the weights and wanting them to move. Those that vary in size will respond to a different tempo. This allows the performer to let people choose the weights that they would prefer to have swing.

Some performers have built up experiments of this type into amazing demonstrations. For general entertainment, however, and particularly with a small group, a single bottle will provide an uncanny enough effect in connection with other spook tricks.

There is a strictly impromptu trick that has points of similarity to the "Spooky Weights." Tie a heavy finger ring or some sort of charm to the end of a thin cord more than a foot in length. Wrap the free end of the cord around your forefinger and thus hold the ring suspended. At command, you can cause the ring to swing sideways, back and forth, or in a circle, halting before each change of direction.

It's done by the same system, the unconscious muscular motion of the hand, and therefore it is good practice in connection with the bottle and pendulum. All you have to do is will the ring to act and it will obey. Do not try to force its motions or your hand will visibly jog. By holding the ring above a drinking glass and watching the glass rim, you gain a mental target that causes the ring to sweep in a much larger circle, without conscious control on your part.

An added feature in this impromptu version of the "Spooky Weight" is that you can let other people try it and they will gain the same results, much to their amazement.

5. The Floating Table

The pastime of "table tilting" has often been regarded as something supernormal by persons who have indulged in it. Even today, there are people who believe that it depends upon spirit aid. A group sits about a table, all pressing hands upon the surface. Soon the table begins to tilt, stopping on the count of numbers or during the spelling of names. It may even jounce about the room, driving some of the sitter's from their chairs.

All this is due to the unconscious action of persons in the group. Once enough pressure has been applied to start the table teetering, a lot of action may occur. The irregular pressure of different individuals is a special factor. It is accountable for occasions when the table indulges in surprisingly eccentric behavior. Yet wild gyrations will not convince the skeptic; unless he sees the table actually rise from the floor against the pressure of the hands, he cannot accept the table's actions as anything too extraordinary.

At times, table sitters have reported that the table actually left the floor, though briefly. This is because one person, then another, have exclaimed that the table is actually floating. Coming from opposite sides of the table, this would seem to be corroborative evidence, whereas the time between the reports—a second or less—is the accountable factor, since a tilt has intervened between. A rotary tilt can cause people all around the table to claim it is in midair. Even when persons on opposite sides give such evidence simultaneously, it proves nothing except that the second person was quicker to call out than the first.

To be convincing, the "Floating Table" should occur during a period of comparative calm, rather than in the excitement of a tilting session. This is where the work of the magician enters. Just to show that tables can float by natural means, he demonstrates it to the satisfaction of his audience.

Two methods are herewith described, each requiring a confederate on the side of the table opposite the magician. The first is a brief, impromptu version. Explaining that all persons present must acquire an equal tension, the magician tells them to place their right hands only on the table, the palms flat near the table edge. Next, each person is told to grip his right wrist firmly with his left band, palm below, thumb and fingers gripping above. The right hands should rest lightly on the table and keep steady.

Suddenly the table rises in uncanny fashion, then descends to the floor. The reason: The magician and his confederate have secretly extended their left forefingers under the right palm and therefore beneath the edge of the table. In this wary, they clamp the table between left forefinger and right hand, readily supplying the lift. Amid the amazement, no one will notice that the magician and the other person are showing only three left fingers each, at the side of the right wrist.

This is simply a modification of the more impressive professional system, which was used by spook fakers until magicians took it over for purposes of entertainment. In this version, all hands are laid upon the table. The magician and his confederate each have a special device strapped to a forearm, hidden beneath the sleeve. This appliance consists of a hollow tube containing a plunger or extension rod.

The other hand secretly draws the rod from its tube, just prior to the placement of the hands upon the table. Hidden by the bands beneath which they extend, the rods become the clamps that enable the table to be lifted. Afterward, these plungers are slipped back into the concealed tubes. Sometimes the performer uses two confederates, so that he can call attention to his own hands throughout the demonstration. Here, the confederates are placed directly opposite each other with the rest of the group between.

6. In The Dark

Reading a book in the dark is an unusual test in connection with a spook act. To make it most effective, nobody should know the particular page which is to be read until afterward. Any book is selected at random and a bookmark is Thrust into its pages. Lights are turned off and soon the performer begins to drone a brief passage. When the lights are turned on again, the book is opened at the marker. The words that the performer spoke prove to be the first sentence on the page.

The trick depends upon the innocent-looking bookmark, which is a strip of cardboard strongly coated with luminous paint. In bright light, the bookmark shows no glow; in fact it is absorbing light. The ends of the strip are not painted; hence when it is inserted in the book, no glow appears when the lights are extinguished.

Picking up the book, the performer turns his back and can even shield the book with his coat, if necessary. Opening the book at the marker, he is able to read from the page by the glow that the luminous paint furnishes. He then closes the book, calls for the lights, and lets the spectators open at the bookmark and check the words the performer read.

The trick can be done without the luminous marker by using some standard book, such as a dictionary. The performer previously places about five pins between pares at the lower end, memorizing the top words on those pages. An ordinary marker is inserted at the top end. In the dark, the performer locates the marker, then opens at the nearest pin and transfers the marker to those pages, giving the words that he has memorized. Meanwhile, all the pins are pulled free and dropped to the floor.

7. Under Cover

·MASTER·

The reading of messages written by the audience rates as a spook trick when performed in the dark; otherwise, this type of demonstration usually comes under the head of mental magic. In the strictly spook version, messages are written on papers which are either folded or placed in envelopes. These are laid on a table beside the performer or an assistant who plays the part of a medium.

When the lights are turned out, the medium begins to read the questions or give their answers, concluding after several messages have been revealed correctly. This is done in a strange voice which produces a most uncanny effect.

Whoever performs the trick uses a dark bag of thin but opaque material. This is concealed on the performer's person or beneath the table where the messages are placed. With the bag is a tiny flashlight. Picking up some of the messages, the performer slips the bag over head and shoulders, tightening it at the waist. With the aid of the flashlight, the performer reads the messages, the bag concealing the glow. The forced voice is used to disguise the fact that the performer's tones are muffled.

You can perform this trick by using a blindfold instead of the bag. Ask a spectator to blindfold you using a 36" square silk. Never use a plastic bag!

Under Cover

8. Catch the Ghost

To produce a gamboling ghost in the center of a group of people, invite them to catch it, and then have it vanish from their very grasp, is something that belongs in the realm of the incredible. Nevertheless, this very effect was produced by the Great Blackstone as a climax to a series of spooky manifestations performed with a committee from the audience.

After working various spook effects iii which the committee participates, the magician announces that he will materialize a full-sized ghost and let the group try to catch it. The committee should consist of a dozen or more men; they are arranged in a circle, with a space toward the footlights, so that the audience witnesses the phenomenon.

When every one is in place and posted to watch for the ghost, the stage lights are completely extinguished. At the magician's command, the ghost suddenly appears. It is a glowing figure of almost human size that spins evasively in the very midst of the circle. The magician then calls upon the members of the committee to grab the ghost and as the men surge toward it, the lights are turned on.

In that instant, the ghost vanishes and the surprised committee men find themselves grabbing each other. Nowhere in the group is anyone clad in ghostly garments, yet it would have been impossible for a person to stow away such a garb in the space of a few seconds. Where the ghost went is as great a mystery as its origin.

Outside of the magician himself, the only man who could give the answer is the "ghost" himself. He is an assistant who comes from the audience, posing as a stranger who has decided to join the committee. At that time, the house lights are on as well as the stage lights, which are not turned off until the time when the ghost is to make its appearance.

The reason for this, is that the assistant is wearing a suit of plain street clothes that has been coated on the back with strong luminous paint, to represent a full-length ghost. This man takes his place toward the rear of the stage, facing the audience, hence his luminous back cannot be seen at the moment when the lights are extinguished.

Immediately, however, the assistant steps forward from his position in the circle and turns his back toward the audience, which immediately sees a shining ghost. In spinning about, the assistant produces a weird effect and is spotted by all the members of the committee. As the rush starts, the lights are turned on, and the luminous effect is instantly ended. The assistant makes a quick dart to one side, clutches the first man he encounters, letting the others grab each other. Thus he resumes his original status as a member of the committee and all are present and accounted for except the vanished ghost.

9. The Spirit Post

This is a device whereby spooky manifestations can be produced by a performer under conditions which make it seemingly impossible for him to operate. A square post, measuring about four by four inches is set upright on the stage, where it stands about four feet high.

One of the performer's wrists is tied with the end of a rope which can be wired to prevent tampering with the knots. The loose end of the rope is pushed through a hole drilled near the top of the post. The performer's other wrist is then tied and wired with the free end of the rope.

The post is already fixed with angle irons, but to steady it further, a guy-line is stapled to the stage, run across the top of the post and stapled on the other side. This line is looped on top of the post and a large spike is driven down into the post to secure the guy-line.

Despite these precautions, the moment the performer is covered with a cabinet, tambourines jangle, bells and horns are blown. All these trappings are in the cabinet with the performer, yet there is no way he could reach them. Any time the cabinet curtain is opened, the performer is seen standing behind the post as firmly tied as ever. Yet the manifestations resume the moment the cabinet is closed again. At the finish, the rope is cut and the performer can show his wrists, still securely bound.

As surefire as it is ingenious, this trick depends upon a special construction of the post, previously, a hole is drilled down through the top of the post to meet the horizontal hole through which the rope is thrust during the binding of the performer's wrists. The vertical hole is fitted with a wooden plug, which has a short, sharp chisel-blade projecting from its lower side. The top of the post is then capped with a block of wood.

The spike used to secure the guy-line is not long enough to reach the horizontal hole through which the rope runs. To avoid suspicion of this, the spike is purposely a short one. But after a few strokes from the hammer the spike is driven through the block that caps the post; encountering the concealed wooden plug, the spike forces it downward when the next strokes are made. The chisel-blade is set at right angles to the rope that connects the performer's wrists; hence the blade promptly severs the rope.

The performer is freed to produce manifestations when the cabinet is closed. Afterward, he must keep up the pretence that his wrists are held together, while the rope is cut at each side of the post to release him from what seem to be untampered bonds. Between manifestations, he pushes the severed ropes back into the hole, thus giving an appearance of bondage every time the cabinet curtain opens.

This act was presented in sensational style by a famous British magician, Doctor Lynn.

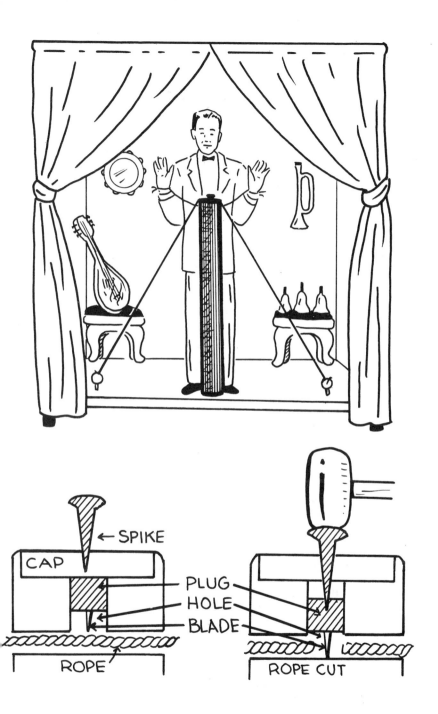

The Spirit Post

10. Seance in the Light

Unlike many spook tricks which were originally used by fake mediums and later adapted by magicians, the "Full Light Seance" was first introduced as a strictly magical effect. Its results were probably quite discouraging to the spook fakers, since it made their "dark seances" seem unnecessary.

However, the trick was soon adapted to comedy acts in which the audience was let in on the secret to gain a laugh at the finish. To gain a really spooky effect, it should be done with slightly lowered lights and included with a routine of so-called "manifestations."

Disdaining the use of a cabinet to encourage ghosts, the performer sets bells, tambourines, slates and other equipment on an ordinary table. He takes a large, thick cloth, unrolls it and holds it in front of the table. The performer is standing at the left of the table, his left hand gripping one top corner of the cloth at his right shoulder. His right arm extends behind the cloth, so that his right hand appears at the far corner of the top, stretching the cloth taut.

Immediately, things happen. Bells ring, tambourines beat. The slate pokes itself above the top of the cloth, bearing a written message in answer to a question from the audience. Later, that message is eradicated and another appears instead. Meanwhile, however, the spooks really cavort. Not merely content with making noise, they fling the bells and tambourines over the cloth. Anticipating this, the performer has provided an extra supply at the start. Nevertheless, when the cloth is rolled up, no sign remains of the mysterious spooks.

The cloth used in this trick has a rod running along its upper edge, within the border of the cloth. Affixed to the far corner is an imitation hand, or rather, a portion of one, representing the performer's gripping fingers. When the cloth is unrolled, this dummy comes in sight, the performer keeping his real hand hidden behind the cloth. Working with that hand, the performer manipulates and throws the bells and tambourines, also writing messages, lifting the slate, later erasing it.

Twisting the top of the cloth backward at the finish, the performer promptly brings up his hidden hand and completes the rolling of the cloth in reverse fashion, the dummy fingers going within its fold.

This spooky demonstration was introduced by Carl Germaine, a famous magician of the Chautauqua and Lyceum stages. Germaine presented it in a highly mysterious fashion, giving it the touch of incredibility treat should accompany a spirit seance. Later it was turned into a comedy act by Frank Van Hoven, the "Dippy, Mad Magician" whose vaudeville act was a burlesque of magic in which he purposely bungled many tricks.

This spirit or seance cloth has many uses. It is available in many different qualities and prices

11. The Hand of Cagliostro

This spooky trophy is introduced as a replica of the hand of Cagliostro, Master of the Occult, but in magician's parlance it is termed a "Rapping Hand." As such, it derives from a device once used in alleged spirit seances, as the replica is supposedly controlled by the long-departed owner of the original hand.

The hand is made of wood and may be examined by the audience. It is placed on a square sheet of glass, which the performer holds by the sides so that the hand is completely isolated. Then, at the request of the audience and the urge of the performer, the hand begins to rap, bringing its fingers down upon the glass with a sharp clack.

Various questions are answered by the hand. It can rap out ages, usually by tens and units. It raps once for "Yes" and twice for "No." At the finish of the actor seance, the hand and the sheet of glass may both be left with the audience, but no one except the performer can cause it to rap.

This mystery depends upon a peculiar construction of the hand. It is made with straight-carved fingers and the hand itself is tilted at an upward angle in relation to the portion of the wrist attached to it. Because of its shape, the hand—with the wrist—is actually a sort of V-shaped balance that teeters on the base of the thumb and the other side of the hand, near the heel.

HAND TEETERS

The hand is hollow and contains a lead weight. The balance is slightly toward the wrist, so when the hand is set level on the glass, it rests back on the wrist. But the slightest forward tilt of the hand will cause it to teeter forward, bringing the fingers down forcibly against the glass. Its tendency then is to teeter back, so with a little practice the performer can keep the hand rapping in sequence. To finish a series of raps, the glass is tilted back just enough to halt the hand when it returns to its original position, resting on the wrist.

By moving about among his audience, the performer minimizes the slight motion that controls the teetering hand, so that it passes notice. He may also hold the hand at the level of his head resting it on his outspread fingers, as if balancing a tray. This position causes the slight tilting motion of the performer's hand to appear quite natural and it is not connected with the mysterious rapping of the artificial band upon the glass.

Effective though this presentation can prove, the method would be detected by anyone who attempted it, as such a person would learn by experiment that the hand was balanced. To prevent this, the hand is equipped with a sliding weight. Pressure on a knob located it the site of the wrist pushes back an interior rod, so that the weight slides back from the hand into the wrist, where it locks in place. This knob, or plunger, is under a velvet band that girds the wrist.

When he lifts the hand from the glass, the performer holds it with the fingers upward, presses the plunger and then gives the hand for inspection with the glass. Anyone who thinks that tilting is the solution, is due for disappointment upon attempting it. The fingers stay upward and the hand simply slides forward from the glass. To start the hand rapping again, the performer holds it with the fingers pointing down and presses the plunger to send the weight into the hand.

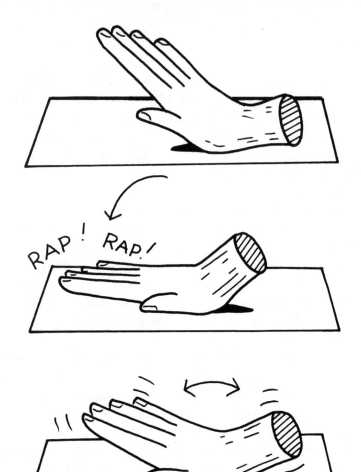

RAP! RAP!

HAND TEETERS

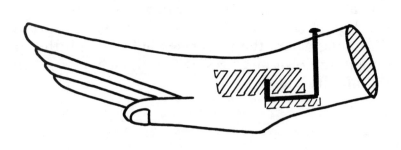

The Hand of Cagliostro

12. Cassadaga Propaganda

This title was used by the Great Kellar to describe a miniature spirit cabinet which was a feature of his show. It was probably coined is a satirical reference to the Spiritualistic colony at Cassadaga, Now York, as though Kellar were promulgating some of the marvels reputed to occur there.

In contrast to huge cabinets and blackened stages which have been used to produce "spook" effects, this miniature cabinet stands out as quite remarkable. Practically every manifestation short of a human-sized "materialization" can be produced within its limited confines. Moreover, it can be worked on a well-lighted stage, under conditions that make the manifestations seem ghostly indeed.

The "Cassadaga" cabinet is about the size of a large cedar chest or a fair-sized trunk, but is of light construction, with a curtained front. It is standing on the stage and in order to isolate it, the magician lays a sheet of glass across the backs of two chairs. He lifts the cabinet, sets it on the glass and shows the audience various objects such as tambourines, bells and slates. The curtains are opened and these articles are placed within the cabinet, after which the curtains are closed.

Manifestations soon begin. The bells ring, the tambourines jangle, writing appears upon the slates. Various objects are tossed out through the open top of the cabinet. Always, when the performer whisks the curtains open, the cabinet is seen to be quite empty. The extent of the phenomena depends entirely upon the amount of time that the performer devotes to this uncanny mystery, which in Kellar's presentation, left the audience in a very creepy state.

Though basically simple, this miniature cabinet has some ingenious points. The manifestations depend upon a person concealed in the cabinet. This explanation seems nullified by the fact that the cabinet is too small to contain one of the magician's assistants. Actually, however, the concealed operator is a small boy, who requires so much less space that his presence is not suspected.

The chairs and the sheet of glass subtly convey the impression that they could not support much weight, whereas the opposite is the case. When the magician lifts the cabinet and sets it lightly on the glass, all doubt regarding a possible occupant is dispelled. This lift, however, is accomplished by the aid of two thin wires attached to the cabinet. These wires, unseen in the slightly dimmed light, run over pulleys above the stage and have counterbalances that neutralize the boy's weight.

The boy goes out through the back of the cabinet, which is hinged for such a purpose, and takes his position on a small shelf. The curtains may be opened to show the cabinet empty. As soon as the tambourines and bells are in the cabinet, with the curtains closed, the boy takes his cue and reaches inside the cabinet to operate the spirit implements.

At intervals, the cabinet may be shown empty and objects replaced within it, only to have the manifestations repeat themselves.

This trick is rarely performed today.

13. The Knotty Spook

·MASTER·

Coiling a length of rope, the performer drops it in a box or small spirit cabinet. He leaves one end of the rope projecting from the top. After a friendly spook has had time to do its work, the performer draws out the rope and the audience is amazed to see a series of knots running its entire length. Since the performer couldn't have tied the knots, presumably his pet spook was responsible.

Actually, the performer ties the knots in the process of the coiling, hence this can be shown as a neat impromptu trick as well as a feature of a spook act. Hold the rope across the palms of both hands, which are palms upward. The rope should be more than a yard in length, but only a few inches dangle from the left side of the left hand, the thumb retaining the rope in position.

The right hand is fairly close to the left, the bulk of the rope hanging over the right side of the right hand, retained by the thumb. The right fingers are bent inward. Then the right hand turns inward and downward to the left until its knuckles are toward the left hand. This forms a reverse loop in the rope, which is placed over the left fingers by the right hand. Moving along the rope to the right, the right hand carries another such coil to the left and continues this process until a series of loose coils gird the left fingers. At the finish, the right fingers reach through the coils and draw the left end of the rope through and out at the right. This end is retained when the coiled rope is dropped into the box.

Later, when the magician draws out the rope by that end, he keeps shaking slightly and the knots automatically form themselves, coming into sight one by one.

For stage work, this effect can be accomplished in convincing style on a highly elaborate scale. Two members of a committee are bound with a long rope, each having an end tied around his waist, the knots even being sealed. The rope, twenty feet or more in length, is so long that to bring the two men close together it must be arranged in coils between them. This is particularly true if the pair are to be confined in a spirit cabinet, but it is logical enough on the open stage, if a blackout is to follow.

After a comparatively few seconds, the men either step from the cabinet or the lights are turned on. As they walk away from each other, a line of knots is seen in the big rope, apparently tied by the knotty spook.

Though the secret is the same as that of the lesser version, it has a puzzling factor; namely, that the coils are not formed until after the ends of the rope have been tied to the committee men. Hence the rope cannot be manipulated by the performer, as it is too unwieldy for such handling.

The trick depends upon one committee man, who is either a confederate or is taken into confidence when he arrives on the stage. As soon as he is in the dark, this man steps into the center of the rope and lifts all of its coils at once, tip over his head and arms. Stepping away he drops the coils on the stage again. When the two men move apart in the light, knots form in the rope in the usual fashion.

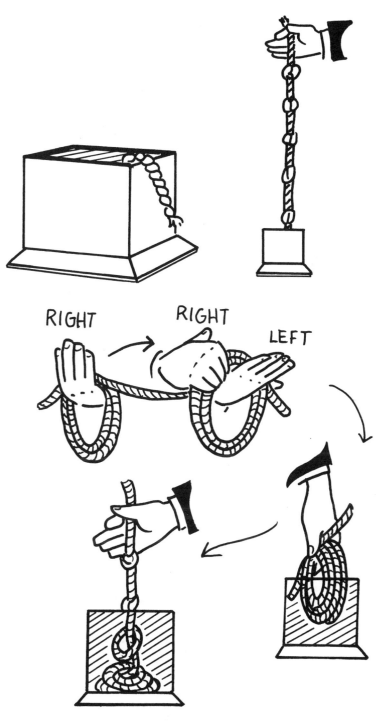

RIGHT   RIGHT   LEFT

The Knotty Spook

14. The Clutching Hand

A routine of spook tricks can always be concluded with a "dark silence" in which weird, glowing objects appear amid the blackness. These can be luminous-headed push-pins in the soles of the performer's shoe, or glowing faces painted on socks which show when the foot is removed from the shoe and swung about. Weird hand-puppets can be employed, coated with the same sort of paint. Such a "spook" vanishes in the darkness by simply turmoil, the costume of the puppet inside out.

Most uncanny of all, however, is the "Clutching Hand" which appears above the heads of the spectators. It is a skeleton hand which makes wild clutches in the darkness, causing people to dodge away from its glowing grasp. Yet the secret of this device is as simple as the effect is uncanny.

Two skeleton hands are pointed on the front and back of a square of cardboard, both being of luminous stuff. One hand is wide open, the other is fisted. The performer also has a thin black stick, a few feet in length, with a split end into which the edge of the card can be inserted.

Extended above the heads of the group, the card shows a glowing skeleton hand of life-size or larger. Immediately, the performer begins to twirl the stick. This brings the fisted side into view, then the open hand again, and so on in such rapid succession that the illusion of a constantly clutching hand is created, adding to its realistic appearance.

Enlargements of this and other devices are used in spook shows presented on the stage, along with other ingenious props, some of huge proportions, which cause such exhibitions to live up to their weird claims.

Stage Illusions

Stage magicians have always presented tricks with large apparatus, not only to gain a greater range of visibility, but because such equipment may be carried quite readily along with the still larger illusions that feature a full evening show. Often, such magic is presented before a curtain, while the stage is being set for an illusion scene.

Thus, in this chapter, the reader will be introduced to certain methods of the great magicians whose careers will be discussed under "Grand Illusions." Many of these tricks were also used by vaudeville performers or magicians who appeared in the concert and lyceum fields, where stage illusions were only occasionally shown.

Tricks with large apparatus have always held their own. Though designed essentially for the stage, they were equally suited to platform presentation and during the upsurge of the nightclub period, many such tricks were adapted to that type of performance. Now, with vaudeville experiencing, its revival and television commandeering all visual entertainment, magic with large apparatus is again in vogue.

Many persons hold to the idea that tricks performed on the stage with large apparatus are easier to do than small, close-up magic. This is an erroneous notion, for the same principles of deception are involved, as the reader will observe by a comparison of the methods. Stage magic actually rates as the more difficult type of presentation, as the performer must have both sufficient talent and showmanship to hold the attention of a large audience.

1. The Flowing Coconut

Presented by Thurston as an Oriental mystery, the "Flowing Coconut" formed a surprising stage effect that rivaled the reputed feats of Hindu magic. Actually it surpasses much of the wizardry of India, for the equipment needed for this presentation would not be available to the average Hindu fakir.

On the stage is a huge bowl, mounted on a pedestal. The bowl is filled with water, as the magician demonstrates. He takes the hollow half of a sizable coconut, dips it into the bowl and pours the water from the coconut. This is repeated several times with increasing rapidity until finally the impossible happens.

As the magician makes a quick, sweeping pour from the coconut, the water continues to flow. It gushes downward in a stream which becomes longer and more apparent as the magician raises the bowl higher. Standing with the coconut inverted, the magician causes the mysterious torrent to continue.

Not only is the coconut inexhaustible; the huge quantity of water that it delivers soon fills the large bowl and causes it to overflow. A cascade surges over the rim of the bowl and floods a trough around the base of the pedestal. The curtain descends with water still streaming from the coconut, as though its supply were perpetual.

Thurston made quite a spectacle of the coconut trick,

but it has been seldom used by other magicians because of the considerable equipment needed for this single feature. The source of the water is a pipe that runs up through the stage, then through the pedestal and finally up through the bowl itself.

This pipe is arranged to deliver a powerful jet of water under high pressure. The coconut has a curved interior to receive the stream. At first, the magician simply dips the coconut in the water which already fills the bowl. In pouring out the water, he inverts the coconut directly over the nozzle of the pipe, which extends to the surface of the water in the bowl.

On the final pour, the coconut is brought almost to the level of the pipe nozzle. That is the cue for an assistant to turn on the water for the pipe, which delivers its full force of water almost instantly. The jet strikes the center of the hollowed coconut, spreads and follows the curve, so that a ring of water gushes downward from just within the coconut's rim.

This not only gives the impression that the coconut is delivering as large a stream as a full-fledged firehose; the circle of downward-pouring water serves as a screen for the upward jet that furnishes the actual supply. The real source of the magical gusher is perfectly masked and there seems no possible way in which the coconut could gain so much water, let alone deliver it.

Since the coconut can keep on pouring as long as the city reservoir holds out, this makes a logical finale for a magic show, as the curtain can be lowered and raised time after time, showing the mystery still in operation. Otherwise, the magician simply gives the cue to cut off the jet. The gush of water ceases and he steps forward with the coconut, showing it to be quite ordinary. The magician tosses the amazing coconut to an assistant and proceeds with more marvels. This trick has faded from popularity.

The Flowing Coconut

2. The Eggs From the Hat

Inviting a boy and girl from the audience, the magician shows an empty hat. From it he begins to produce eggs, handing them to the girl and instructing her to give them to the boy. More and more eggs keep coming from the hat. Soon the boy's arms are so laden with eggs that he can scarcely hold them.

The eggs then begin to drop. The girl becomes so busy placing the eggs in the boy's arms and steadying those already there that she enters into the spirit of confusion. Meanwhile the magician is blandly producing eggs in inexhaustible style. At last, the remaining eggs are salvaged and the trick brought to a mysterious as well as laughable conclusion.

Presentation is the essential factor in this trick. The hat is a special one of double construction, with an inner lining that conceals the eggs, which are packed all around the interior. Through an opening in the lining, the magician draws out the eggs, depending upon the quantity of the eggs to give the mystery its zest.

The "Eggs and Hat" was a specialty with the Great Raymond, who performed it throughout the world. Raymond's rendition was particularly artistic because of the way in which he kept passing the eggs along to the girl, who failed to see the next egg as she reached for it, in her anxiety to make sure that the boy did not drop the heap that was precariously balanced in his arms.

Thus the girl, not the boy, was the one who dropped the eggs and at the finish, Raymond would carefully work the eggs from the boy's arms back into the hat, so skillfully that the audience would gain the amazed impression that more eggs had been produced than the hat itself could have held.

This was real artistry in contrast to the way in which many performers worked the act, their procedure being to hurry the boy into dropping so many eggs that the stage was spattered with them. This was an inferior presentation, as it reduced the trick to a comedy number and nothing more.

In Raymond's hands, the "Eggs and Hat" soon became a feature of his show and stands out as a striking example of magical accomplishment.

With the passing of popularity of men's hats, you can use a plastic hat available at the party stores or even a paper bag (see illustration). This is not a trick to try in your parents' living room!

FALSE BOTTOM

The Eggs From the Hat

3. The Fade-Away Glass

This mystery was a favorite with David Devant, the famous English illusionist, who performed many of his marvels in a deliberate and convincing style which added to the mystification of the audience. It illustrates how a comparatively small trick can be built to a strong magical climax.

The magician shows a large glass, considerably larger than the average tumbler. He fills it with water, covers it with a cloth, and approaches the footlights. At this point, the audience expects the glass to be vanished from the handkerchief, but the magician is not so abrupt about it.

Coming down the steps into the audience, the magician lets them hold the glass within the handkerchief, making sure that it is really there. He taps the glass through the cloth and people hear its muffled ring.

By now, everyone is impressed by the fact that the glass is quite a large one, since people themselves have handled it. Obviously it would be quite a task for the magician to conjure away such a sizable glass of water in the midst of his audience. When he places his hands beneath the handkerchief, every one supposes that the magician merely intends to bring out the glass and give the spectators another look at it before returning to the stage.

Instead, the magician suddenly whisks away the handkerchief and the glass is gone. He tosses the handkerchief for examination, shows his hands completely empty, takes a bow and returns to the stage, leaving every one with the impression that the glass literally faded away.

There is an adage that "nothing should be done by halves" but the rule does not apply in magic. The glass used in this trick is actually of double thickness, consisting of a bottomless outer cylinder around a straight-walled glass. After filling the apparently normal glass with water, the magician covers it with the cloth and lets the inner glass drop into a bag behind a table, the water going with it.

Thus the glass that the spectators feel beneath the cloth is only the outer cylinder, but it is of the right size to pass as the glass. When the magician places his hands beneath the handkerchief, the large size of the cylinder proves a help, not a handicap, for he is able to slide it over one hand and well up his arm, beneath his sleeve. That is the last place where the audience would suspect a large glass to go, particularly as they suppose it to be filled with water. Thus the rapid vanish is as baffling as it is unexpected.

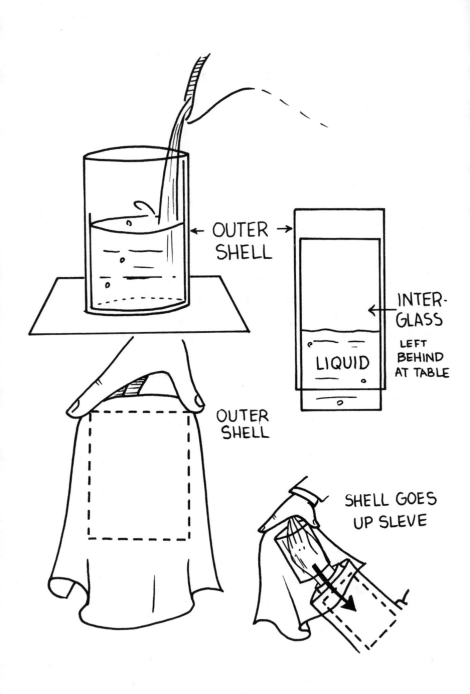

The Fade-Away Glass

4. The Imaginary Keg

Famous among feats of magic is the "Inexhaustible Bottle" from which a great quantity of liquid is poured, but such a mystery is quite outdated by the "Imaginary Keg."

In this impossibility, the magician plays entirely upon the imagination of the spectators. He begins by showing a sheet of cardboard, about two feet square, which is embellished with a drawing of a keg. He places the cardboard upon an easel or skeleton stand, then calls attention to the fact that there is a hole near the bottom of the keg, obviously intended for the insertion of a spigot, or tap.

The magician provides such a tap. It is exactly the size of the hole, so he fits it in place. Then he requests the audience to imagine that the keg is a real one. Turning the tap on, the magician provides a flow of liquid that fills a large glass. As the magician hurriedly brings up another glass, it too is filled. More glasses follow until, from the imaginary keg, the magician has filled as many as half a dozen glasses.

Naturally, the liquid must come from somewhere, so the audience supposes that there is a tank behind the cardboard that is resting on the stand. But when the magician removes the tap, be shows that the cardboard is quite innocent of any preparation, while the stand, being of skeleton construction, is equally tree of trickery.

The liquid must come from somewhere in order to flow out of the tap. The place that it comes from is the tap itself. Outwardly the tap appears to be a simple wooden plug, some six inches in length and less than three in diameter.

Actually, it is made of thin metal, hence it is quite hollow and contains the liquid which is due to flow from the imaginary keg. When the tap is inserted in the hole in the drawing, a good portion of it goes out of sight, hence the spectators never realize its full size.

This, however, is only half the trick. While the hollow tap contains a surprising amount of liquid, it is scarcely more than enough to fill one of the glasses that the magician uses, provided those glasses were as ordinary as they appear to be.

Special glasses are used. Each has an inner cylinder, sealed at the top. The space between the inner cylinder and the outside of the glass is reduced to less than half an inch. Being of glass or transparent plastic, the inner cylinder is not visible. Hence when the magician fills a glass, the liquid flows around the inner cylinder. The glass can be shown from all sides, apparently filled with liquid.

The special glasses so reduce the amount of liquid required in proportion to an ordinary glass, that the magician is able to fill half a dozen or more of them from the special tap. This in itself diverts suspicion from the tap, which is removed and laid aside. Then the sheet of cardboard and the skeleton stand may be shown quite freely, leaving the observers baffled as to the source of the mysterious flow.

The Imaginary Keg

5. Fish from the Air

Featured by Chung Ling Soo in an act of Chinese magic, the art of "Aerial Fishing" stands out as a distinct novelty. An audience is always intrigued when a magician performs something extremely unusual, and the fishing trick—by virtue of its effect—most certainly fulfills that qualification. Though other performers, such as Horace Goldin, have also presented this mystery, it is most effective when introduced in an Oriental setting.

Taking a long fishing pole from an assistant, the magician attaches a hook and sinker to the end of the line. Swinging the line out over the audience, he makes a sudden cast and catches a wriggling goldfish on the hook. Rapidly reeling in his catch, the wizard removes the fish from the line and drops it into a bowl of water where it swims about.

Putting another hook on the line, the magician makes another cast and catches a second fish which is also added to the bowl. He repeats this until he has caught as many as half a dozen fish, all from the thin air above the first few rows of the audience, who find themselves staring upward in search of more invisible fish that have somehow been materialized from nowhere.

The "fish" are contained in the sinkers which the magician attaches to his hook. These weights are actually small hollow tubes. In each is a piece of silk cut to the shape of a goldfish and similarly colored. The strips of silk themselves are slightly weighted, and rolled up in the tubes, to which they are attached by cords.

A quick shake of the rod causes a silk "fish" to drop from the tube, unroll, and wiggle lifelike on the line. In the handle of the fishing rod, the magician has some real goldfish, confined in separate compartments supplied with small wet sponges or paper to keep the fish alive. As he catches each fake fish he obtains a real one from the rod handle. Gathering in the line, he detaches the silk and sinker with the hand that contains the real goldfish, which he promptly drops into the bowl, the sinker along with it.

The swimming goldfish catches full attention in the spotlight while the metal tube and the strip of silk sink unnoticed. Baiting the hook again, the magician continues the aerial fishing until he has used up the supply of real fish in the rod handle. The trick gains effect by repetition, particularly as the increasing number of fish in the bowl convinces the audience that they are viewing something marvelous.

Chung Ling Soo used to "explain" the trick to interviewers by telling them that he snagged the mysterious fish from a bowl that was hidden up the copious sleeve of one of his Chinese assistants, Inasmuch as the hook never went near the assistant, the people who thought they had learned the trick were all the more puzzled when they went to see it again.

When Goldin presented the aerial fishing, he varied it somewhat by carrying a large box which bore the printed word "Bait" in big letters. The supposed bait that he took from the box and attached to the hook before each catch was simply the usual bit of tubing containing the silken imitation fish.

6. Houdini's Giant Bowl Mystery

This effect was presented by Houdini at the famous New York Hippodrome during one of the seasons that he appeared there. Worked near the footlights, it was well suited to such a large auditorium. The items used, combined with the effect itself, resulted in a convincing production.

Houdini began by showing a solid sheet of glass set in a metal frame. This he placed on top of a square, ornamental table. Next, he exhibited a huge glass bowl, practically a giant fish bowl, which he placed upon the frame of glass. The bowl was filled with water and therefore could be seen to be devoid of trickery.

Into the water, Houdini poured a concentrated fluid that gave the water the blackness of ink. Dipping his hands into the bowl, he brought out quantities of silk streamers which continued to appear in almost endless array until the stage all about him was strewn with yards upon yards of silk which had to be gathered by assistants.

Though the bowl was filled with liquid, the streamers appeared dry and their source of origin was most mysterious, considering that the bowl was isolated from the table by the intervening glass. As a finale, Houdini gathered a mass of silk and from it produced a live eagle, the only trained bird of its species, which settled on the magician's shoulder.

Typical of much of Houdini's work, the Giant Bowl Mystery depended largely upon showmanship, though the method, despite its basic simplicity, had the necessary elements to puzzle the audience. The table was of the conventional magician's pattern, with velvet-draped top and gold fringe, and though much sturdier than the average, did not appear overly bulky. This table was actually a sort of box, containing the well-packed streamers, which could be reached through a masked opening in the table's top.

The bowl had a hollow center, composed of a large, watertight glass cylinder. It could not be seen inside the bowl due to the refraction of the water. The cylinder was open both at top and bottom and was large enough for the magician to reach down through. The sheet of glass was made to slide in its frame, in the fashion of a drawer, so after the bowl was set upon the frame, the sheet of glass could be drawn back, unnoticed behind the bowl.

Thus, when the water was darkened, Houdini reached down through the bowl and pulled up the silk streamers, which had their ends looped to form a successive line. The quantity of silk was tremendous and made a line showing. This aided in the final production, because while the audience was watching Houdini, one of the assistants, gathering up the silk, had plenty of opportunity to obtain the eagle, which was in a bag located elsewhere.

When the streamers were brought to the magician for a complete display, he released the eagle from within the bundle, thus topping a remarkably]are silk production with an unexpected sequel, giving the impression that the eagle, like the silks, had emerged from the mysterious bowl.

This trick is typical of the large stage magicians of the early twentieth century. Simple to construct, this illusion can be a great opener or closer for any show. The eagle can be replaced with a dog or cat. The finale can even be a bouquet of flowers.

7. The Great Sack Escape

Escape tricks come under the head of stage effects, although they may be performed in various other places, even at the bottom of rivers. However, they figure in a magical show only as a special added attraction, because it is difficult to estimate the time they will take. They are more in the category of a challenge than that of strict entertainment.

To perform escapes requires a great deal of practice and foresight, for the work is both arduous and dangerous, and is suitable only to the practicing professional who must find some way to advertise his show through sensational publicity. Such performers will find all sorts of people challenging them to escape from anything from bank vaults to refrigerators. Such feats can become quite troublesome and strenuous, though often some very imposing escapes prove far less difficult than they appear.

Since escapes are useful only to a limited number of performers, there is no purpose in going into a catalog of complicated devices. What the average performer needs is a good escape that impresses his audience, yet avoids danger as well as the necessity of carrying bulky paraphernalia. Hence "The Great Sack Escape" is recommended, particularly because it is as easy of performance as it is ingenious in method.

The performer introduces a large black sack, which may be thoroughly examined. He is placed in the sack and a borrowed handkerchief is tied around the neck as proof that the performer cannot cut the bonds that hold him, since the handkerchief is to be identified later. Next, ropes are tied around the neck of the sack above the handkerchief; to identify these, they may be sealed with wax.

The performer is then placed in a cabinet. After a short interval, he appears before the audience, carrying the sack, with the knotted handkerchief and the sealed and knotted ropes still intact around the neck.

To work this mystery, two sacks are required. They are identical in appearance and it is best to have them made of fairly thin material, because they must be packed in small space. At the outset, the performer has one of these sacks folded and tucked under his coat. The other sack is examined by the audience and the magician gets into it.

The magician has an assistant helping him and here is where the assistant's work comes in. The assistant gathers up the neck of the sack, holding it rather loosely and starts to tie a borrowed handkerchief around it. By then, the performer has removed the duplicate sack from beneath his coat. He thrusts the neck of the duplicate up through that of the original sack.

Adjusting the sack necks, the assistant ties the handkerchief tightly around the spot where they join. The sacks being black or of other dark material, this trickery with the necks is not observed and the handkerchief hides the join adequately. The assistant keeps pulling it tighter while spectators—brought on stage as a committee—tie ropes around the neck of the sack above the join. Actually they are tying their ropes around the duplicate sack—not the original. These are the ropes that are later sealed.

To all appearances the magician is tightly imprisoned in the sack. Once he is placed within a cabinet or behind a screen, he has no trouble with his escape. He simply peels away the outer sack (the original) leaving the handkerchief as well as the ropes tied around the duplicate. Folding the original sack, he tucks it under his coat, hiding it as the duplicate was hidden in the first place. Then the performer makes his appearance before the puzzled audience, bringing along the duplicate sack, which can stand any amount of examination.

This escape must be well rehearsed beforehand and care must be taken in handling the committee, as is true with the majority of escapes. Those precautions taken, "The Great Sack Escape" will prove to capital mystery. As an escape it will be found well suited to a magical show because it can be performed quite rapidly, without the long stage waits that have made many escape tricks too slow and tedious for presentation before modern audiences.

The Great Sack Escape

8. Canary and Light Bulb

Taking a canary from a cage, the magician apparently tosses it at a glowing electric light bulb which is in a table lamp. Instantly, the light goes off and the canary is seen inside the glass bulb, which must be removed and broken open to release the bird. The bulb is of the nonfrosted variety, hence the canary's arrival is visible and as sudden as the extinguishing of the light.

Two bulbs are used, one ordinary, the other containing a canary. They are fitted in a double socket, each portion at right angles to the other. The lighted bulb points straight downward, coming in sight beneath the rim of the lampshade, which conceits the bulb with the canary inside.

The socket is on a swivel, operated by a spring the instant a release cord is pulled by an assistant. This causes the lighted bulb to swing up to the horizontal, while the bulb containing the canary swivels down to the vertical, thus replacing the lighted one. A cutoff extinguishes the lighted bulb and it remains hidden beneath the shade, as the canary bulb originally was, but pointing in the opposite direction.

The bulb containing the canary is of course a special type that comes apart, but it is broken open with a hammer to make it seem ordinary. Two canaries are used; the magician merely pretends to take the first from its cage, actually trapping it in a compartment in the cage bottom.

From the mechanical standpoint, the lamp used in this trick is a fine example of magical ingenuity. It was devised an constructed by Carl Brema of Philadelphia, whose son

Will has carried on the manufacture of the precision-built apparatus for which his father was famous. The original lamp was made for Horace Goldin and later was featured by Howard Thurston, through a mutual arrangement.

9. Fish Globe Production

The production of a bowl of goldfish from beneath a cloth is always highly effective during an opening routine, particularly in conjunction with other productions. Since a fish bowl is anything but collapsible, the audience is much impressed when the bowl arrives from nowhere; moreover, upon seeing the bowl, the spectators are inclined to believe other production objects are also solid and bulky.

Originally, goldfish bowls used in productions were small and quite shallow, more in the style of fingerbowls. Such bowls were covered with broad rubber caps and could thus be hidden beneath the coat, held in vertical position. By reaching beneath a cloth, the magician could obtain the bowl,, bring it level, peel away the rubber cover with the cloth and show the bowl.

To make a more sizeable production, a special type of bowl is now used. This bowl is of the familiar globe variety, the sort in which goldfish are usually sold. With the greatest of ease, the wizard reaches beneath a cloth and brings out a fish globe some six inches high and of proportionate diameter. He sets it on the table, letting the fish swim merrily about while he proceeds with further productions.

This globe is not all that it appears to be. It is constructed to give a maximum of display, while occupying a minimum of space. It is only half a globe, as viewed by the audience and even less than that from the magician's viewpoint.

To the front half of a fish globe is added a crosswise partition, forming the back of the half-globe. This partition, however, instead of being straight, is curved, but not as sharply as the front portion of the globe. Thus, viewed from above the "globe" forms a crescent, its convex lines toward the front.

The fake globe is made of plastic or celluloid, so that it is transparent and can hold water. Goldfish swim in the narrow space between the two curves. The bottom of the globe is abbreviated, simply connecting the front of the globe with the curved false back. Attached to the rim of the false back is a celluloid tab, which can be hooked down over the magician's vest pocket. Since the back of the globe follows the curve of the performer's body, the globe is readily concealed beneath the coat, showing no betraying bulge.

To produce, the magician's free hand lifts the globe beneath the coat, automatically releasing it. The globe is then brought from beneath the outspread cloth and held on display, care being taken to keep the curved front directly toward the audience, so that the globe appears to be an ordinary one.

The bottom of the special globe should be slightly slanted, rising from front to back. Thus the globe can be set on the table and will stand there, adding to its authentic appearance. When the globe is removed by an assistant, he should bundle up the cloth with it, keeping the cloth bundled around the back of the globe, so that the missing portion will not be discovered.

Fish Globe Production

10. Aquarium Production

Even more amazing than the production of a fish globe from beneath a cloth, is the appearance of a full-sized aquarium upon a table less than half its height. As with the fish globe, the magician makes this startling production under the cover of a large cloth.

The aquarium looks genuine enough, being of rectangular shape and containing a considerable quantity of goldfish. However, as with many magical properties, its appearance is deceitful. The main portion of the aquarium is simply a thin front, consisting of two walls of glass a few inches apart, closed at the top so the water will not escape. The fish are between these walls of glass.

Hinged at the bottom, this false front lies flat upon the table and springs up when released. The sides of the aquarium are simply flaps of metal, painted to resemble water and goldfish. These spring upward and outward in the same fashion as the front. Underneath the front and sides is a shallow pan of transparent plastic filled with water which can be lifted straight upward from within the table, locking the false front and sides of the aquarium in place.

The whole device is covered by a velvet drape which appears to be part of the table top. Under the cloth, the magician pulls away the drape, catches the hidden tray and lifts it, bringing the front and sides of the aquarium upright. He carries the drape away with the cloth and with his free hand splashes some of the water in the tray to prove that the aquarium is as genuine as it appears to be.

The size of the table top is naturally reduced after the appearance of the aquarium, but this only adds to the illusion. It is impossible for the eye to gauge the size or depth of a table top without something by way of comparison. Seen beforehand, the table top looks much smaller than the aquarium, as in fact it is. After the production, it appears to be even smaller and the only object with which it can be compared is the aquarium itself.

Moreover, the actual drape should be gathered under the table beforehand. There it is held in place by little clamps which in turn are connected to the false drape, which the magician removes beneath the cloth. Thus the removal of the false drape releases the genuine one, so that the table top—though smaller and shallower—looks exactly the same after the aquarium has made its magical appearance.

11. Duck or Rabbit Production Box

The production of two or three live ducks from an empty box is always a sensational effect. Where the ducks come from is a problem to the audience; how to keep them there until their appearance is the magician's problem. This type of box answers both problems satisfactorily.

Picking up an oblong box with an overlapping top and bottom, the magician grips a handle on the top and lets the box drop wide open. The front side of the box is hinged to the top, the bottom of the box is hinged to the rear side. Thus the box opens accordion fashion, letting the audience see clear through it.

The box is closed by simply raising the bottom upward, gathering the box proper and clamping the lid shut. When the magician opens two doors in the top, the ducks appear and hop out, quacking loudly, to waddle across the stage.

In the description of the box, we find the answer. Apparently the box is shown entirely empty; actually, it is not. Attached within the top of the box is a container, almost as large as the box itself. In opening the box, the magician swings the top forward and outward; thus the container can not be seen. When he lifts the box, the hinged center drops and from it dangles the bottom. The eyes of the spectator follow the dropping box and observe that nothing is concealed in the main portion or the bottom.

Nobody suspects the innocent looking top behind which the ducks are concealed in their container. In closing the box, the magician takes care to bring the bottom up toward the top, which is allowed to settle in place without revealing the load behind it. The reason for the double doors in the top is now plain. Upon release, the ducks come out of their container, through the top of the box.

A few more details should be noted. The doors in the top should fit neatly, one having a strip that overlaps the other so that the ducks cannot be glimpsed, Also, the doors should be held together by a catch, so that the ducks cannot force them open too soon. Those points observed, the trick is certain of operation.

This box can also be made in smaller size for the production of a rabbit or other objects Such as silk handkerchiefs and spring flowers. When made in smaller proportions, a single door in the top is quite as effective as a double door. It should, of course, be a good fit and have a catch.

The beauty of this production lies in the bold, direct handling of the box. The magician should simply pick it up by the handle, which is attached to one of the doors (or the single door in the case of a smaller box). If picked up from a tray or table, the box opens automatically. If the magician holds his other hand beneath it, he can let the box drop apart whenever he chooses. A good clear view convinces the audience that the box is entirely empty and the magician has only to close the box and proceed with the production.

Since its inception, this same box with two holes, one on one on each side of the box, it has been used mainly for vanishes and is called a "flip-over" box.

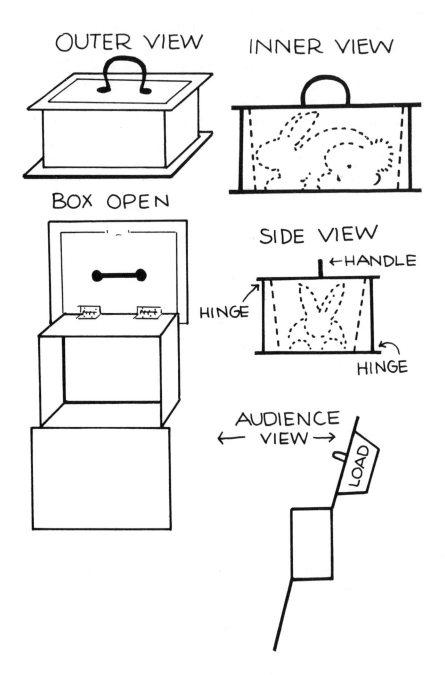

Duck or Rabbit Production Box

12. The Flying Cage

A large, square birdcage is shown to the audience and is covered with a cloth by the magician. Carrying the covered cage forward, the magician rests it upon a skeleton frame, cubical in shape, which is just slightly larger than the cage. The skeleton frame is mounted on a thin pedestal, completely isolating it. When the cage is rested on the cubical frame it is set at an angle, so its full shape is outlined beneath the cloth.

Taking the sides of the cage between his hands, the magician lowers it into the frame, beneath the cloth, where the metal of the cage makes a pronounced clatter. The cloth, descending with the cage, now covers the frame as well. There is no possible way to remove the cage from the skeleton frame unnoticed. Yet when the magician whisks away the cloth, the cage has vanished, the birds with it.

Unknown to the audience, there is a second skeleton frame, slightly smaller than the one on the pedestal. There is another difference: the special frame is bottomless, whereas the visible one has a solid bottom. The smaller frame fits over the birdcage quite snugly and is not noticed, because it appears to be the framework of the cage.

After covering the birdcage and its unsuspected loose frame, the magician lifts it backward from a draped table and lets the cage drop on a padded shelf behind the table. The special frame, however, retains the full shape of the cage. It is set askew on the larger frame to represent the cage. After lowering the supposed cage into the larger frame, the magician has only to whisk away the cloth, as the edges of the smaller frame are within those of the larger and match them exactly.

13. The Pop-Through Frame

This is a production trick with a surprise feature. Devised by Milbourne Christopher, it is an example of portability in equipment, enabling magicians to carry considerable apparatus in small space.

An assistant brings on a large square frame which the magician covers with a sheet of paper. As the magician calls upon the audience to name colors, the paper punctures itself automatically and through the hole pops a large silk handkerchief of the first color called.

This is repeated, colored silks arriving from nowhere in the order given by the audience. The wizard can also cause flags of various nations to make their "pop-through" appearance as demanded.

Over his right hand, the assistant wears a hollow dummy hand, which he attaches to the side of the frame. Inside his vest or jacket, the handkerchiefs, flags or both are arranged in careful order. The frame is quite large, extending at least a foot on each side of the assistant. The assistant can draw his right hand, unseen, from within the hollow dummy.

While the left hand alone supports the lightly constructed frame, the hidden right reaches into the vest, draws the required silk from its place and gathers it against the back of the paper. The finger punches the silk through the paper, causing it to pop into sight, the finger being gone from view before the silk drops clear. Other silks are similarly produced, as called. At the finish, the right hand slides back into the dummy.

Easier than a fake hand would be the use of a thumb or a dye tube. These are both easy to obtain.

Mentalism

The latest development in the realm of the mysterious is that of "Mental Magic" which has also been publicized under the high-sounding title of "Mentalism" with the performer termed a "Mentalist" instead of a mere magician. Various factors have been responsible for this, so to give the reader a perspective of the subject, they will be treated here in brief.

Originally, mental effects were introduced in an act styled "Second Sight" wherein a magician glanced at objects proffered to him by members of the audience and called upon a blindfolded assistant to name them, which was done with surprising accuracy. Codes, signals and other systems of secret communication were utilized in this type of magic by various famous magicians until finally performers appeared upon the scene who specialized in such work only.

Most notable of such performers were the Zancigs, who titled their act "Two Minds with but a Single Thought" and astounded scientists and other investigators throughout the world. The Zancigs so elaborated their work that it was undetectable even by persons acquainted with the ordinary systems. Thus the Zancigs set the pattern for present-day "two person" acts which have been developed even further and require months and even years of practice and performance to approach perfection.

For a long while, the "Second Sight" act appealed chiefly to the intellectual members of a magician's audience. This was because a surprising percentage of the population, particularly in isolated districts, were inclined to accept many of the illusions that they witnessed on the stage as something akin to real wizardry. When Harry Kellar was bold enough to depict imps and demons on his lithographs, he did so in the face of arguments that such advertising would scare away a considerable percentage of the public. Even Howard Thurston, who succeeded Kellar and used similar billing, received complaints from persons (who were daring despite their superstitions) on the ground that devils did not appear in the show as pictured.

Feeling the public was sufficiently educated to accept magic as an art, legitimate magicians emphasized their skill at sleight-of-hand and described their stage effects as "illusions," even soft-pedaling their ever-popular Spook Cabinets as "anti-spiritualistic phenomena." The public, still wanting to believe in the impossible or miraculous, began to accept "Second Sight" as something psychic, since neither skill nor mechanics seemed capable of explaining it.

This led to a high-pressure type of performance that was practically the hokum of the crystal seer's parlor transferred to the theater. Self-styled "Mind Readers" sprang up in abundance and flourished through the vaudeville era. Foremost in this cavalcade was the celebrated Annie Eva Fay, whose act was extensively copied and elaborated. In such performances, questions are gathered from the audience, burned or otherwise destroyed, after which the mind reader "sees" the questions in the crystal and gives the answers.

Either the questions are "switched" for dummies, or facts are gained through the use of pads prepared to give the equivalent of carbon impressions. In any case, they are listed for the mind reader and supplied to him along with his crystal or by a variety of other devices. Through stooges or local informants, the act is given exaggerated proportions and the main purpose is to delude the gullible.

In contrast, the "mental tricks" performed by magicians come under the head of legitimate entertainment. This was the case with their "anti-spiritualistic phenomena" of years ago. But the very public which now regards such things as "Spirit Slate Writing" as nothing more than trickery, is charmingly inclined to grant supernormal ability to the purveyors of so-called "mental tests" that depend upon strictly magical methods.

This is simply the result of catch-phrase education. Wise-acres watching a magician will say, "Up his sleeve," or "It's done with mirrors," to explain away the disappearance of anything from a coin to an elephant. The actual case is that modern science and invention have managed to beat home the fact that physical impossibilities do not happen. But the marvels of the mind are still unexplored and the easiest way for ignorant persons to explain some feat of mental wizardry is to accept it as genuine.

The vast majority of observers never analyze magical effects beyond the point of guesswork. Otherwise they would recognize that the skilled sleight-of-hand man, who can vanish a coin before their eyes, might just as readily pluck a written question from an envelope without detection. They won't believe the magician who says that through some hypnotic power gained in India, he is literally able to saw a woman in half without harming her. But they will ,swallow the mentalist's patter when he declares that by tuning in on thought waves, he can gain impressions from concentrating minds.

This is unfortunate. It has enabled mediocre performers to command more public interest than skilled sleight-of-hand artists who have spent years perfecting their technique. The same applies when a mental show is extended to two-hour length before a theater audience; it lacks the colorful dramatic quality found in the performance of a stage magician, with his fanciful settings and intriguing apparatus.

Mental magic is therefore best suited for impromptu performances or fair-sized audiences. With the latter, the performer can often work his impromptu tests with the aid of a committee. In many instances, the performer concentrates upon mystifying individuals, counting upon their bewilderment to impress the audience as a whole, a factor which must be played up always. This is not different from other magic; often a magician will borrow a coin or a watch from a spectator, vanish it, and have it reappear to be identified solely by the owner. But with mental tricks, working for individuals is as much the rule as the exception.

Contrarily, the major purpose is to produce a mass amazement. To achieve this, a performer may often turn a stranger into a temporary confederate, letting him in on the secret of a trick—or a part of it—in order to astound the audience at large. Such subterfuge has been used with other types of magic, but very rarely. However, it has long been professional policy not to worry about a few persons catching on to a trick if everyone else is baffled.

These factors understood, you should not be surprised at the bold simplicity of the mental mysteries that follow.

1. Message Reading

·MASTER·

Basic among feats of mentalism is that of "Message Reading" in which the mental wizard answers questions that have been written by members of his audience. The simplest and most direct process is to have such questions folded and dropped into a hat or basket. From this receptacle the performer plucks them one by one, holds them to his forehead and gets reasonably correct "impressions" which he answers.

The time-honored system of performing this mystery is called the "One Ahead," a highly descriptive term which practically reveals the method. The performer holds one question to his forehead, gets only a vague impression. He opens the paper, finds that its question is illegible or unimportant, so he lays it aside. Taking another slip, he gets a definite impression, gives the answer, then opens the paper and reads the question aloud to show how accurate he was.

Actually, the performer merely bluffs with the first paper. Upon opening it, he reads the question written on it, but only to himself. He pretends that the question was trivial or too scrawly to read, because he is actually saving the question for the next slip that he draws from the hat. That's why he answers the second question so well. When he opens the second slip, he reads off the question that was really on the first. Meanwhile he is memorizing a fresh question which he can answer when he holds the third slip to his forehead.

This stunt is very hard to beat. It was a favorite years ago with fake "psychics" and "fortune-tellers," and the small-timers in such trade still use it extensively. Magicians often neglect it as too elementary, partly on the assumption that keen members of the audience may catch on to the process. Actually it is extremely convincing when sold in serious style by the charlatans who demonstrate it regularly.

When working at a table, the performer simply places each opened question beside the hat or basket. When pretending to read the next question after opening it, he reads from the one that is lying before him. By having a confederate in the audience, the performer can make the first answer a real convincer by addressing his comments to the stooge, who of course corroborates everything the performer says. With a large audience, such a confederate does not put a question in the hat at all. With a small group, he should mark the outside of his paper or fold it in a peculiar style so that the performer can pass it up until it is the last slip in the hat.

This "One Ahead" system can be applied to questions that are sealed in envelopes. In this case, the performer opens each envelope, takes out the question and pretends to read it aloud, as usual reading the one just ahead. Done as an impromptu trick, particularly among friends, this form of "Message Reading" should be done rapidly and with humorous answers. The routine should also be cut short rather than risk too many speculative comments from the audience who are likely to be skeptical as to the mind reader's powers.

This illusion, made famous by talk show host Johnny Carson, is a really cute effect

2. Single Messages

Very effective is the trick of reading a sealed message written by a member of the audience, then handing him the envelope and letting him open it for himself. This is particularly strong when it can be repeated, as is the case in this method. In fact, the several envelopes which are passed around can even be initialed by the spectators, precluding all possibility of substitution.

One precaution is important. The slips of paper given out with the envelopes should be cut to a size slightly smaller than the envelopes themselves. People are told to write questions on the papers, tuck them into the envelopes without bothering to fold them. Otherwise—though he doesn't mention it—the performer will encounter complications. That brings us to the important factor in the case.

The performer has a large stack of envelopes from which he distributes some in which the spectators can peace their written slips. Only about half of the envelopes are genuine. The rest are glued to form a dummy stack. Not only that, the stack is hollowed out and inside it is a flashlight of the square type which resembles a miniature electric lantern. In working this trick today you can obtain a small flashlight that will light when you squeeze it. Either that, or the flashlight is rigged specially to fit inside the dummy stack.

Lying flat in the stack, the flashlight has its bulb in the center, pointing upward. As a precaution against giving this device away, the flashlight may be hidden by a thin strip of paper pasted across the opening above it. The bottom of the dummy stack is of course firm and solid, being reinforced with cardboard like a box.

The envelopes should not be very large as the purpose is to reveal their contents in X-ray fashion by using the gleam of the flashlight. This is done as follows: In gathering the real envelopes, the performer places them on the bottom of the stack, holding the stack upside down so the bottom looks like the top. The real envelopes go below the dummy. Drawing one envelope off and holding it to his forehead, the performer lets his hand turn over with the stack.

Now, when the envelope is brought away from the forehead and briefly laid there, it comes just above the hidden flashlight. Keeping the stack turned toward him, the performer presses a concealed switch. The light glows through the envelope, enabling him to read the writing on the paper within it.

Drawing away the envelope, the performer gestures with it, holds it to his head again and finally answers the question or reveals whatever words he saw on the paper. He returns the envelope to its owner, unopened. Then he proceeds to read another question in the same fashion. This is continued until the performer has read as many questions as he desires. Sometimes of course he encounters "confused thought impressions" but that is only when he meets with a folded or poorly written slip.

In this trick, it is advisable to have considerable distance between the performer and his audience. Also, the performer should be fairly well surrounded by lights. Such details are essential so as to prevent the spectators from noting any strange glow emanating from the neighborhood of the performer's hand. Fake mediums would attribute that to ectoplasmic phenomena, but we are considering the subject strictly in terms of magical entertainment.

Single Messages

3. The Untouched Card

When a performer manipu-
lates a pack, it's Magic; when
he reveals a card without
touching the pack or even
seeing a person take a card,
it's called Mentalism. All of which adds up to Magic, which
is the superlative in all events, whether or not a trick
happens to come in what seems a purely mental category.

Two packs are used in this trick, or "test," as it is commonly called. The performer hands one to a spectator, has
him run through the cards faces up, showing them to the
audience. The spectator may also shuffle the pack if he
wishes. The performer meanwhile runs through his pack
in the same style, displaying a variety of jumbled faces.

Then to make all fair, the performer takes the pack which
the spectator shuffled, giving him the other pack in exchange. Placing the pack he has just received face downward in his left hand, the performer tells the spectator to
do the same. The magician then states that he wants the
spectator to cut somewhere about the middle of the pack,
and lifting the upper group, to look squarely at the bottom
card of that group. He is to note and remember that one
card only, taking care to observe no others. Then he is to
replace the upper portion of the pack back on the lower.

The magician illustrates this with his pack so there can
be no mistake. At the same time, he restrains the spectator
by saying, "Not yet!" Having conveyed to the spectator just
what he is to do, the magician sends him to the far corner
of the room, so he can note a card while his back is turned.
The spectator may step outside the room if a door is handy.

Upon the spectator's return, the performer tells him to lay his pack aside. Not once does the magician intend to touch it. He wants the spectator simply to think of his card and think hard. During that process, the magician runs through the pack that he is holding and finally draws a card from it. He tells the spectator to name his card aloud. This is done and the magician triumphantly shows the drawn card to the entire audience. It is the very card that the spectator named, after noting it in the other pack!

This minor miracle is accomplished very simply. At the start, the magician has a "Forcing Pack" in which a batch of the cards are exactly alike. In the old days, such a deck contained fifty-one identical cards with an odd card for the bottom. This particular pack has only about half its cards identical, but they are sandwiched between two groups of indifferent cards, top and bottom.

While the spectator is running through an ordinary pack, the magician casually does the same with the "Forced Pack." He slides cards openly from left to right until he has displayed about a dozen, then with his left thumb he pushes over the bulk of the cards and continues his slow, emphatic exhibit with the last dozen cards at the top.

This is the pack which the magician plants in the hand of his helper, taking the ordinary pack in exchange. When the obliging volunteer cuts to somewhere near the center, as the performer illustrates, he just can't miss getting one of the "Forcers." When the man returns, the performer has him lay that pack aside. From the ordinary pack, the magician draws out the necessary card and the trick is as good as done. Careful attention to detail and dramatic effect are the elements that build the mystery.

4. Duplicated Thought

Slates are popular items with the mental worker, as any writing on them appears clearly and can be erased later, like a fleeting thought. Yet there are times when those thoughts are not as fleeting as they might seem. Such is certainly true in this instance of a duplicated idea.

The mentalist passes a slate and a piece of chalk to a spectator, requesting that he hold the slate so that he alone can see its nearer surface. Beside the spectator, the performer places a moistened sponge or cloth. Then, while the performer is a considerable distance away, he asks the person to write any initials, figures or geometric design that he may wish.

During the writing, the performer avoids glancing at the spectator. He suggests that the written item be shown to a few trusted persons for later verification. He asks the writer to concentrate upon the inscription for a period of about a dozen seconds. Then, sure that he has caught the impression, the performer tells the spectator to obliterate the writing with the sponge.

That done, the performer takes the slate, shows it all about, proving that the surface is damp and clean. He lays the slate aside, concentrates a short while and finally takes the chalk and begins to mark something on the state himself. Finally, the performer asks the spectator to name what he inscribed, that is, the mental image which he still retains. As soon as the description is given, the performer turns the state to the audience.

There, in exact detail, is the performer's reproduction of the very thought which the spectator put in chalk, only to eradicate before the performer could have seen it.

Apparently this demonstration precludes all chance of trickery, particularly where the slate is concerned. Indeed, the value of slate tests lies in the fact that in many instances the slate is comparatively innocent. In this case it is completely so, though it plays a part. The article upon which success hinges, yet which passes totally unsuspected by the audience, is the chalk.

This particular chalk has previously been soaked in oil, which gives a greasy effect to anything it writes. This is so slight that it escapes detection and when the slate is cleaned with a damp cloth, the oil impression is temporarily eliminated against the deep blackness of the slate. Rubbing with a dry cloth would not be sufficient and would have a tendency to smudge. But the water has no effect on the oil, though it does render it unnoticeable for a brief time.

That brief time is the period required for the slate to dry. Therefore, the performer must go through a few attempts at concentration unless he is combining this test with another and is picking up some other person's impression first. When the slate is dry, the performer naturally uses it to register his own thoughts and in the light he sees a thin, dim replica of whatever his victim wrote.

Over this product of the oil slick, the mentalist chalks his own impression which cannot fail to duplicate the original inscription.

Through the years new and improved impression slates have been invented. They are a big improvement over this old method.

5. Color Clairvoyance

Announcing that he has experimented in identifying colors through extrasensory perception, the performer offers to demonstrate this to his audience. So far, he says, he has not been able to develop his peculiar powers beyond the primary colors of red, yellow, and blue, but they will suffice to prove his ability.

Handing the audience three small wooden cylinders shaped like candles, the performer calls attention to the fact they are painted red, yellow, and blue. He also exhibits three silk handkerchiefs of those colors and places them in a hat, where they are stirred by a spectator.

Meanwhile, someone places one of the colored cylinders in a metal tube provided for that purpose. The other two cylinders are hidden. It is preferable that the person should not note the color of the cylinder used, since this is an experiment in clairvoyance, or discovering hidden objects, rather than an attempt at telepathy.

Taking the tube, the performer hands it to another person. He then reaches into the hat, which someone holds above his head. From the hat, the performer draws a handkerchief, for example the blue one. The tube is opened and inside is found the blue cylinder. Thus the performer has duplicated the colors and to prove that luck was not the factor, he repeats the experiment several times, always drawing out the handkerchief whose color corresponds to the cylinder found in the tube.

If he wishes, the performer may do this test blindfolded. To add interest during the repeats, it is a good idea to introduce the blindfold after the experiment has been done a few times. This counteracts any lurking suspicion that the performer may somehow glimpse the cylinder or the handkerchief.

This interesting demonstration is an elaboration of a divination trick known as the "Patriotic Rockets," a term applied to the candle-shaped cylinders, which are made of painted wood. The "rockets" contain small metal weights. When the tube is held in the center, between thumb and forefinger, the direction of its tilt reveals the color. Red is toward the tip of the tube; yellow balances; red tilts toward the base. Usually, the rockets are red, white, and blue, but it is better to use yellow for the intermediate color. Being pointed at one end, the rockets cannot be inserted the wrong way, as the metal tube is shaped in the same fashion.

The three silk handkerchiefs are specially prepared for the trick. In a corner of the red silk, a tiny round bead is sewn. A comer of the yellow (or white) silk contains a square bead of similar size. The blue silk has a small cylindrical bead, like a bit of tubing, sewn in one of its corners.

These beads are not noticed in handling—the handkerchiefs, particularly if the performer holds the silks by those corners before dropping them in the hat. Anyone mixing the silks about will not encounter the beads. But the performer, reaching into the hat as it is held above his head, has simply to feet for the corners until he finds the one that designates the proper color. He has learned that color, of course, when he hands the metal tube containing the rocket from one spectator to another.

6. Out of the Phone Book

As a mental effect, this comes in the "prediction" class and therefore belongs to a type that many mental wizards introduce to lend variety to their performance. After all, if a mentalist can "read minds" in the present why should he not be able to project his uncanny power to the revelation of a future thought? The answer is that he can, provided of course that his audience is gullible enough to believe that his mental tricks are something more than magic.

In this instance, the prediction involves a name seemingly taken at random out of a phone book. The larger the phone book the better, because it makes the trick easier. This will be understood from the explanation, but for the moment, it merely emphasizes the fact that something other than chance dominates the "random" selection of the name.

To start, the performer invites three or four people to serve as a committee to observe that all is fair. The use of that many helpers not only makes the demonstration more effective; it also facilitates the working of the trick, as will be detailed later. Looking over the committee and remarking that he is in a predictive mood, the performer writes something in crayon on a large piece of cardboard. Keeping the written side away from sight, he lays the cardboard on a table or props it against some object. In any case it is placed well out of reach of the committee.

Taking a phone book, the mentalist flips through the pages and hands a person a calling card. He asks the person to push the card somewhere among the pages. To assist in this, the performer holds the book with its end toward the spectator telling him to thrust the card half way or more into the pages. The performer turns to another spectator, asks him to take the phone book and open it to the exact spot indicated by the card, then to pick which page he wants, the one on the left or the one on the right.

While the second spectator holds the book open, a third man is asked to stop forward, hold his hand above the indicated page and place his finger anywhere he wants, without looking at the names. The performer then reads off the name thus indicated, which we will suppose is George Q. Lewis. He reads the phone number and street address aloud. This emphasizes that the name has been chosen utterly at random. However, the phone number and such data are inconsequential. The performer states he simply wants everyone to remember the one name: Lewis.

Then, closing the phone book, the performer proves that be had foreseen this exact situation. He asks someone to pick up the large card and turn its written side toward the audience. There, in big letters appeals the name "Lewis" which was inscribed by the mentalist before he even offered the phone book to the committee.

Stupendous though this demonstration may seem, it is merely an exaggerated form of a basic "Book Test" that was popular with alleged mediums who flourished in the days when "Spirit Slate Writing" was popular. Use of the telephone book, rather than a smaller volume, permits of a few embellishments that build up the effect. First, the performer must manage to "force" the particular page he requires. This is done with the aid of a duplicate calling card, which is first placed between the proper pages, so that it projects about half its length from the lower end of the phone book.

This card is near the binding, hence it is not seen when the performer runs through the pages, particularly as he keeps one hand cupped over it. When a spectator is asked to insert a calling card, the performer proffers the upper end of the book, still keeping the other card concealed. In turning to another spectator, the performer places his other hand over the upper end of the book and simply changes hands, at the same time pushing the upper card out of sight among the pages.

With this hand, the performer lowers the book and when he raises it again to give it to the spectator, the only card in sight is the one originally planted at the lower end. Using that as a bookmark, the committee member opens the book at that point and the force is made.

Stress is now laid upon the choice of either page and the blind picking of a name. This is where the bulky size helps. In the directories of larger cities, many names—like Lewis— occupy two complete pages or more. A few odd names in the upper left or lower right do not matter, as choosers invariably ignore the corners. Of course the performer reads the full name, as George Q. Lewis, but gradually drops all except the one name Lewis, before revealing his prediction on the cardboard.

It is always best to choose a name that people will not generally suppose will be found in such frequency. A study of any of the larger directories will disclose those that are most suitable.

With the elimination of binding on phone books, this same effect can be accomplished using any large book or even an unabridged dictionary. You can simply predict the first word on the page.

7. The Marked Name

Showing a large slate, the performer holds it upright and asks people to call out names at random. These may be simple first names: John, Mary, or whatever anyone may call. They may be names from a group, such as those of presidents or famous men—even cities or countries.

As the names are called, the performer writes them on the slate so that they form a column of some eight or ten names, with a space at the left. Now he asks that a committee decide upon which name is to be used for an experiment in mental concentration. The committee may even retire to another room and attempt to project the thought from there.

In no case is the mentalist to be given any inkling of the name. He faces the audience, holding the name side of the slate toward himself. Running his hand up) and down the slate, he hesitates here and there, finally announcing that he has marked an "X" in front of one of the names.

The committee then is summoned and is told to announce the chosen name. We will suppose that it is "Margy," at position seven in the column. Calmly, the mentalism turns the slate around and shows the "X" at the left of the name Margy, proof absolute that he plucked the thought of the committee through some process of Mental Radio.

Quite convincing, this trick, yet very simple of execution. The trick lies in the slate, which is specially prepared for this. The slate is furnished with a flat square of metal, painted jet black, like the surface of the slate. On this metal tab is an "X" painted in white to resemble a chalk mark.

The metal tab extends from beneath the frame at the left of the slate. The end beneath the frame is fitted in a groove. At the very edge of the slate proper is an upright pin, attached to the tab. All the performer has to do is run his thumb up and down the edge of the slate frame and the metal tab will slide along. The pin is set at the bottom edge of the tab, so the metal square can be pushed out of sight under the top frame of the slate, which is furnished with a slight space to receive it.

With the metal tab hidden at the start, the slate is quite ordinary in appearance. After writing the names, the performer goes into his moments of concentration and makes a great show of hesitancy, as though starting to mark an "X" at one spot and then another. He can also pretend to make a mark, then rub it out. All this is to prevent the audience from guessing where he actually puts the "X" mark. As a matter of fact, the performer makes no mark at all. He simply announces that he has done so; then, without showing the name side of the slate, he awaits the verdict of the committee.

When the name is stated, the performer is holding the slate with both hands, his left thumb at the upper left corner, pressing the pin. As he steps forward, he draws his thumb down to the chosen name, bringing the marked tab to the right position. Releasing his right hand, he turns the slate around with his left, showing the "X" in front of the name. Being black against black, the metal tab is never noticed or suspected.

The maneuver is natural and no more than momentary. It is never noticed because of the motion of the slate which the performer can be lowering, then turning, as he is stepping forward. As an added throw-off, the performer can be holding the chalk between the fingers of his right hand, on the near side of the slate. This not only attracts attention; if the name is far down the list, the performer can draw the tab part way, then lay the chalk aside with his right hand. After that, the right hand again grips the slate long enough for the left thumb to complete the adjustment of the tab.

Immediately afterward, the performer rubs out the names with a cloth. During this process he pushes the tab up out of sight beneath the upper frame. Thus when the slate is shown it is entirely blank, the "X" mark apparently having been erased with the names.

This trick has an advantage in that it can be performed as an experiment in thought projection instead of reception, thus fitting with different styles of programs. As a projection test, the mentalist states that he will pick a name and send it mentally to the committee, or preferably to some individual chosen by the audience.

The performer asks the recipient—or receiving group—to announce the name which made the strongest impression. When the name is stated, the mentalist turns the slate around and shows that he marked that very name.

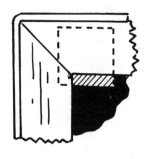

The Marked Name

8. The Random Mind

·MASTER·

Purveyors of mental wizardry are frequently called upon to present some impromptu demonstration of their wares under conditions that will suit the most exacting skeptic. Nothing could be more convincing than letting the skeptic himself choose a total stranger with whom the mentalist is to perform an experiment in telepathy. That is exactly what happens in this case.

While the effect may be presented during a regular performance, it is more suitable for a small group, as in a restaurant, hotel lobby, or anywhere that strangers may be available. Taking a note book and pencil from his pocket, the performer requests the skeptic to pick out some friendly-looking person who might be willing to test out the mental waves. Such a person is invited to join the group and the performer tears off a sheet of note paper, folds it twice and hands it to the stranger along with a pencil.

"I would like you to take this paper some distance away," the performer says. "Then turn your back, unfold the paper and write a number of three figures. Understand, I want a number of three figures to be written on the paper; then fold it and bring it back to me. At no time are you to speak a word to anyone. Is that agreed?"

The friendly stranger nods, goes away with the paper and pencil. Concentrating, the performer writes a number on another sheet of paper, using another pencil. He folds this paper and drops it in a glass or lays it beneath a match pack. The stranger returns and the performer tells him to place his paper in another glass or beneath another match pack. When the skeptic opens the two folded slips, he finds that each bears the identical number.

On the basis of one chance in a thousand, this result seems uncanny, but the performer is dealing with a person, not a number. On the bottom surface of the top sheet of the pad, the performer has previously written a number, say 388. When he folds the paper, he does so in downward fashion. Hence the folded paper that he hands the stranger actually has a number written on it. That number, however, has not been seen by anyone.

When the stranger retires with the folded paper, he opens it intending to write a number. To his surprise, he discovers a number already there and he begins to catch on to the part that he is to play. As an added hint, the performer has given him a pencil without an eraser or a point, so the stranger can neither rub out the number nor inscribe a new one.

Being that far in the game, the stranger's tendency is to play it through. He folds the paper and brings it back. Meanwhile, the performer, disguising his writing, is putting down the number 388 on another sheet of paper, which he folds. Having been told to say nothing, the stranger simply places his paper where told. When it is opened, its number corresponds with that on the performer's sheet.

Bold though it is, this flimflam has just the twist that leads to its success, particularly when demonstrated by a clever operator. In his wording, his request for strict silence, the performer is selling the stranger on the idea from the start. If the stranger has a pencil, the performer may even borrow it, then lend the man his own, which makes it all the more pointed—but not the pencil!

Should the stranger refuse to cooperate or give the thing away, the performer can brush it off as a joke, even stating that he tried it just to prove how difficult it is to influence a person into becoming a confederate. This however is something that will very rarely happen. About the only hazard is that the stranger may not catch on and may prove dumb enough to return, saying a number was already written on the paper.

To avoid that, the performer can have a little typewritten slip, telling the spectator just what he is to do, which includes putting the direction slip in his pocket. Or the slip can tell him what number he is to write, saying that the stunt is just a game on the party. Such a slip is already tucked beneath the top sheet of the note book when the performer tears it off and folds it. But the experienced performer can sell the idea without relying on this added subterfuge.

This clever device has been attributed to the celebrated "Doctor" Reese, who for years convinced his clients that he was a genuine telepathist. The final stage of the game is to thank the stranger and politely get him to bow out of the picture. This is not too difficult, but it is claimed that Reese took no chances on that score. It is said that his system was to fold a dollar bill inside the paper and have the skeptic pick a bellboy or a waiter as the stranger in the test. In accepting and pocketing this tip, the impromptu stooge would find it good policy to remain silent.

9. In The Crystal

MASTER

Crystal balls are commonly associated with mind reading and clairvoyance. Usually it is the mentalist who gazes into a crystal to learn the answers to questions that his audience has offered. In this case the situation is the opposite and therefore quite astounding. Stating that he will project a mental image of a playing card previously chosen by the audience or selected at random, the performer lets a spectator gaze into a crystal ball and see the answer. Without a word from the mentalist, the spectator names the card, much to the amazement of the audience and sometimes to his own bewilderment.

The secret is simple but effective. The performer has a tiny playing card printed on thin paper. This little slip is moistened and placed on the ball of the thumb. In picking up the crystal, the performer transfers the slip to the glass ball, which should be at least three inches in diameter. He places the crystal in the spectator's hand so that the little card is at one side.

Now, by simply lifting the person's hand, the card comes into sight through the crystal and is not only magnified but appears to be an image within the crystal itself. When the person names the card he saw there, the performer takes the crystal, sliding off the little card with his thumb. In presenting the trick in full, he ether forces a playing card on the audience or pretends to take one at random from the pack. The notion is that by having the entire group concentrate on that card, the man with the crystal will gain its mental image in the ball. If a susceptible person is chosen, he is often more impressed than the remainder of the audience.

10. Calling All Cards

This begins as an astounding mental mystery and finishes as a comedy stunt; but each depends upon the other, as will be evident from the explanation.

Stating that he will cause any spectator to become a mental marvel, the performer asks the audience to choose the person that they want, specifying only that a man be designated. This done, the performer places the man in a chair facing a corner of the room.

Taking a pack of cards, the performer tells the audience that he will show them one by one and that the man in the corner will catch the thought waves and name the cards. Showing the top card, the performer asks its name and the man says "Three of Hearts" which is correct. Showing the next card, the performer asks its identity and is told "Seven of Spades." This also is correct as are the next cards shown, until the volunteer assistant has named as many as a dozen cards in a row.

This is just the first part of the demonstration, but before proceeding with a description of the sequel, it is advisable to explain the mystery so far.

In placing the spectator in the corner, the performer asks him to rest his hands in front of him. Into the man's hand the performer puts a card which says:

Let's work a stunt on the crowd. When I ask you to name cards, call them as follows: Three of Hearts, Seven of Spades, Jack of Diamonds, Four of Clubs, Two of Diamonds, Ace of Spades, Nine of Clubs, Jack of Hearts, King of

Spades, Eight of Clubs, Ace of Diamonds, Queen of Spades. After that, put this list in your pocket and say nothing.

The performer has memorized the list of cards and has them on top of the pack in that order. Invariably the volunteer assistant will enter into the spirit of the thing. As the performer shows the cards and asks their names, the stranger calls them.

That's all there is to it, but it can prove very amazing. However, if the trick ended there, people would ask too many questions, particularly of the stranger. So the performer switches immediately to the comedy sequel.

Stating that he would like to test another thought recipient, the performer asks that a woman be chosen. She is placed in the corner, but is given no list. Shuffling the pack, the performer places his finger to his lips, requesting the audience to preserve silence. He then starts showing cards, asking the woman to name them.

Since the lady is only guessing, she names each card wrong, but every time the performer announces "Correct" and again gestures for the witnesses to remain silent. When he says "That's enough," the woman will immediately exclaim that she simply called each card as it came to mind and is more amazed than anyone else because of the result.

By then, the whole audience will be laughing and the lady will soon catch on to the joke. Afterward, however, people will begin thinking back and wondering how the man who first played "assistant" managed to hit every card as called. As a result, the performer will be credited with having performed a very amazing mental test before lapsing into a bit of humor.

11. Nailed Thoughts

· MASTER ·

Announcing that he will present an experiment in sheer telepathy, the performer produces a new, scaled pack of cards and requests that the pack be opened, then shuffled thoroughly by several persons present. The pack is then wrapped in a piece of newspaper and placed upon a board. A nail is driven through the pack and deep into the board.

Turning his back or standing some distance away, the performer tells a person to tear the newspaper and draw cards from the top of the pack, one by one, ripping them from the nail. The person is to look at each card as it comes free and the performer will catch the thoughts instantaneously. This is exactly what happens. One by one, the mental marvel calls off the names of the cards as the person rips them free and notes them.

This is an excellent example of the claptrap that can turn a simple trick into a pseudo-miracle. All that the performer requires is a dozen extra cards to match the new pack that is used. These extras are arranged in an order which the performer memorizes. They are placed in the center of a folded sheet of newspaper. The other half of the paper is then folded over to conceal the cards and a few dabs of paste or wax are applied outside the corners of the cards to keep them in position. The doubled paper is then creased, close to the edges of the hidden cards.

After a new pack has been opened and thoroughly shuffled by different persons, the performer asks someone to look through it and remove the joker or any advertising cards. The joker is laid face down on the table; then the pack is given another shuffle and is placed face down on the joker. The performer introduces the sheet of newspaper, holds it on his hand and asks that the pack be laid in the center, face up, the joker preventing anyone from seeing the other cards in the pack. The pack is then folded in the paper, which is turned over, placed on the board and the nail driven through.

Now, when the paper is torn and the top cards ripped from the nail one by one, the cards actually come from the special packet between the double layer of paper. The performer calls them off in order, stopping the process before the group is exhausted, so that the person does not reach the layer of paper separating the group from the actual pack. Since the pack is now useless, the performer tosses it aside, board and all, along with the ripped cards. This disposal is natural and no one ever thinks of examining the mutilated cards as a clue to the mystery.

The performer must be sure to hold the prepared paper so that its concealed cards are face upward when the pack is placed thereon. Adherence to this precaution avoids about the only pitfall that might be encountered. Of course a pack of cards is ruined, but the result is worth it.

A bolder method of adding the extra cards is to have them in the coat pocket. After the pack has been repeatedly shuffled, the performer palms the extras from his pocket. Receiving the pack with his free hand, he squares it, face down, adding the extra cards, and promptly sets it on an ordinary sheet of newspaper so that the pack can be wrapped and nailed to the board. In the hands of a skilled worker, this is never detected. New packs of cards are always less bulky than those which have been used; hence the addition of a dozen more cards does not make the pack look too thick.

12. Nine Out of Nine

Though more of an impromptu effect than a deep-dyed mental mystery, this can be used with a committee, with very good results. It also has advantages as a "preliminary test" to learn if a person is in the "mental mood" for a serious telepathic experiment.

The subject is given a sealed envelope, which he is told contains some cards. He is then asked to write a number, containing as many figures as he wishes: three, four, five, or even more. This may be written on the envelope or a pad of paper. He is then told to reverse the number, figure for figure and to subtract the smaller from the larger.

For example: The person writes 38224. Reversed, this is 42283. Subtracting 38224 from 42283 leaves 4059. But the process does not stop there. The person is told to add the figures in the remainder, which he does. In this case, they would total 18. He is told that if the total comes to more than I 0 (which in this case it does) he is to add the figures again. In this instance, I and 8 will give him 9.

None of this calculation is noted by the performer but it may be checked by another spectator. The performer then hands the subject four tiny boxes, asks him to take his choice, open the box, and note the color of a tiny block or wad of paper that he finds inside. The subject does this and finds—for example—a red block.

Opening the large envelope, the performer shows that it contains a batch of blank cards of different colors, such as red, yellow, green, and blue. Running through those cards,

the performer shows that the reds predominate, number-
ing more than all the rest together. In fact, the red cards
representing the chosen color—total exactly nine, which
was the lone figure that came from the elaborate calculation.

People aren't always willing to accept this even as a coin-
cidence. They have a habit of looking into the other boxes
to find out if they contain red blocks too. But they do not.
The remaining boxes contain blocks of yellow, green and
blue respectively, and the result is a real mystery.

Inasmuch as the properties used in this trick are easily
obtained, a careful study of the details will enable the reader
to try it out at very short notice. If it sounds complicated at
first reading, remember that its complexities are all planned
as part of the game, which is to confuse the spectators. Actually, it all cracks down to a simple process.

The number nine is the key. Any number of several figures, reversed, with a subtraction following, will give a number whose figures add up to a multiple of nine (such as 9,
18, 27). Where two figure numbers are concerned, they
will reduce to nine when the figures are added. So the performer is sure of that part.

Now for the matter of the cards. There are exactly twelve
cards. Nine of them are reds, so if red proves to be the
chosen color, the performer has only to open the envelope,
spread out the cards and show that there are exactly nine
red cards, though each of the other colors is represented
only by a single card.

The ninth card from the top of the packet, however, is
the green card. So if green should be the chosen color, the
performer says nothing about the total number of red cards.
Instead, he counts off the cards one by one and shows that
the ninth from the top is a green card, the only green one
in the lot.

Fourth from the top of the packet is the blue card. If blue happens to be the chosen color, the performer simply turns over the envelope before he opens it. Thus when he counts down to nine, the blue card is the one that turns up at that number.

This leaves only the yellow card to be considered. It is the top card of the packet. On its under side is written the word "Nine" in bold letters. In the previous examples, in weeding out nine red cards or counting down nine to the green card, the cards are not turned over. Hence no one realizes that there is anything written on the yellow card. In the case of blue, the count ends before the performer reaches the yellow card; but after showing the blue card at position nine, he should absently turn over the three remaining cards before spreading them to show there is no blue among them. Again, the writing on the yellow card will remain unrevealed.

Should yellow be chosen, however, the performer first turns over the envelope. He then removes the cards and shuffles them before spreading them out. Somewhere in the batch, the yellow card will show up, hearing its bold message of "Nine."

This trick would be a good one if it worked nine times out of ten. It does better than that; it works nine out of nine. No need to worry about the tenth time—it can't happen.

13. Relayed Thought

Most performers of mental magic enliven their routine by using some unusual methods of revealing the thoughts that they have garnered from the audience. Inasmuch as the mentalist does experiments in thought projection as well as reception, it is logical that he should be able to convey one person's thought to another, with the performer himself acting solely as a relay.

The method about to be described serves that purpose, though it may be reduced if desired to an experiment in straight thought projection, as that is the part in which the trick device is used. However, the combination is more effective, so "Relayed Thought" will be given in its entirety.

Some gentleman in the audience having noted the serial number of a dollar bill, or taker a card from a pack, the performer extends a short rope and asks that the gentleman take one end of it, the performer holding the other end in his left hand. Taking another length of rope, the performer retains one end in his right hand and asks a lady to hold the loose end.

Now the performer asks the gentleman to concentrate upon the first figure of the bill, which he may be holding in his free hand. As the performer counts steadily from one to nine, adding zero if necessary, the gentleman is to give a mental command of "Stop" when the right figure is reached. The lady is instructed to stay "Stop" aloud, should she gain any impression or impulse at the announcement of a certain number.

As the performer counts, the lady suddenly says, "Stop"—at the number five, for example—and the gentleman nods that it is the figure on which he concentrated. This is repeated again and again, the lady stopping the count on every figure of the dollar bill's number. Sometimes the performer goes through the entire count, telling the lady to name the impulse number when he finishes. The result in this case will be the same. Similarly, the performer can call off the name of a playing card, first by suit and then by value, and the lady will get the mental impression.

If a dollar bill is used, the performer simply borrows one from the audience and switches it for a bill of his own—the number of which he has memorized—before handing it to the man who is to work in this experiment. In a case of a playing card, it is forced on the gentleman, who is serving only as a blind, since he really has no part in the trick.

The lady is therefore the important factor. On that account, the performer gives her the end of a special rope. This rope is a casing over a rubber tube that has a bulb at one end, a tiny bag of thin rubber at the other. The bulb is hidden in the performer's hand; the "palpitator," as the thin bag is termed, is in the rope itself, at the end which the lady holds.

When the performer secretly squeezes the bulb, the palpitator expands and supplies a slight, mysterious pressure within the lady's hand. Accepting this as the expected impulse, she halts the count at that point, or remembers that particular number. Having no idea of the cause, she supposes it to have something to do with a mental impression.

Information gained from a scaled message—such as the month, day, and year of a birth—can also be relayed in this fashion.

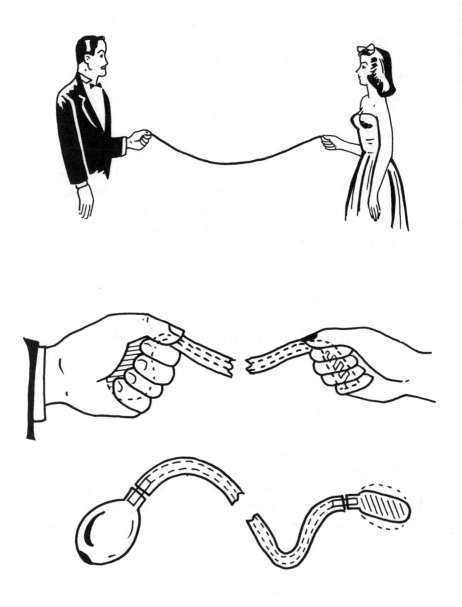

Relayed Thought

14. The Mental Challenge

Presented under so-called "test conditions," this demonstration apparently defies all laws of probability, unless telepathy is accepted as the answer. Of course the performer himself sets the conditions—which is commonly the case in such tests—but they are so exacting that they leave no room for improvement or argument.

What the mentalist purports to do is read a message direct from the minds of a specially-chosen committee, or a single member of that group. The message may be a sentence, a quotation, or merely a group of words. The person doing the concentrating may be in another room, or at some distant point. The message itself may be brought sealed in an envelope. If the person is absent, he is told the time at which to concentrate, or is informed at the proper moment by messenger or telephone.

All being ready for the challenge, the mentalist has the committee choose some person as a judge. The committee sits at one side, the judge at the other, with the mentalist between. Capturing the thought upon which the committee—or some absent person—is concentrating, the performer writes it on a sheet of paper and hands it to the judge. He then asks that the sealed message be opened and read aloud by the committee. This is done.

For example, the message might be: "In summer the tree leaves are green." As soon as it is stated, the mentalist turns to the judge and asks him to read aloud the words which he—the mentalist—wrote on the sheet of paper. The judge does this, announcing that the entire message is absolutely correct. This forms a remarkable climax to a performance of Mental Magic and convinces the audience everything that went before was quite as marvelous.

The great feature of the Mental Challenge is the absurd simplicity with which it is accomplished. If the performer can induce the participants to follow his instructions to the letter—something to which they agree beforehand—he is leaving nothing to chance. All he needs is a sincere committee and a serious-minded judge, plus a lot of bluff.

Everything is done to convince the audience and particularly the committee that this is to be a genuine feat of mental concentration, practically a scientific experiment, and with nothing prearranged beforehand. Thus interest has been built to a high pitch when the time comes for the performer to receive the mental message. Impressively, the mentalist writes something on a sheet of paper, which he promptly folds.

But it is not the message that the mental wizard claims he has caught through thought waves. All he writes is this simple statement:

"The entire message is absolutely correct."

Handing this folded paper to the judge, the mentalist tells the committee to open the envelope and read the original message. They do this and announce that the message says: "In summer the tree leaves are green." Telling the judge to open the paper that he holds and read what he finds there, the mentalist calmly awaits the result. The judge reads what he sees on the paper: "The entire message is absolutely correct."

Everyone takes this as confirmation of the performer's claim that he had divined the original message when he wrote his own. Only the judge is "in the know" and his conclusion is either that the mentalist decided to introduce some humor into the act, or that through some failure in the test, he is trying to pass it off in a light manner. The judge has fulfilled his part; there is no reason for him to spoil the show.

This bold stunt, however, has a tricky sequel. While the judge is opening the paper and reading it, the performer puts his hand in his coat pocket and uses a short pencil to write on a small pad "In summer the tree leaves are green" (the original message which the performer now knows). Tearing off that sheet, he folds it in his pocket, like the paper from which the judge is reading the "answer." Concealing this in his hand, the performer steps over to the judge, takes the paper from him and smilingly says he will give it to the committee. In walking over, he exchanges papers, so the one the committee receives actually bears a copy of the original message.

Taking it for granted that this was the paper from which the judge read, the committee is totally nonplussed, while the judge, watching their reactions, assumes that they are merely feigning amazement to help the mentalist out of a dilemma. That is why this act should climax a mental show, because the performer's next job is to shake hands with the judge and bow him out one door while the committee is leaving by another. After that, spectators usually crowd around to look at the original message and compare it with the "duplicate" that the mentalist wrote.

The greater the build-up to this stunt and the stronger it is sold, the less likely is anyone even to imagine the simplicity of the expedient whereby it was accomplished.

Grand Illusions

The spectacular period of magic began shortly before the present century with the introduction of the great stage shows which have continued ever since. At that time, the leading magician in America was Alexander Herrmann, styled Herrmann the Great, an amazing wizard of Mephistophelean appearance who toured the country in his private railroad car, carrying a company of assistants and tons of baggage.

It was Herrmann who first emphasized the large-scale art of the illusionist in contrast to the ordinary style of stage magic, the distinction being that stage illusions consist of magic performed with living people or huge objects, rather than small or inanimate objects. Herrmann vanished ladies, floated them in air, and even produced a huge array of animals from an empty Noah's Ark that took up a goodly proportion of the stage.

When Herrmann died suddenly in 1896, he was succeeded by his nephew Leon, who adopted the title of Herrmann the Great and copied his uncle's style and makeup for a decade. Later a nephew by marriage styled himself Felix Herrmann and carried some of the Herrmann tradition clear into the 1930s. This explains why many people today claim to have once seen "Herrmann" though the original Great died before their time.

Herrmann's greatest rival was Harry Kellar, who became America's leading illusionist until 1909 when he announced Howard Thurston as his successor. Thurston enlarged the show far beyond the size of Kellar's and toured for more than twenty years with a full evening performance, frequently introducing new illusions or reviving old ones.

During those years, many other magicians were rising to fame as illusionists, mostly in the vaudeville field. Among them was Harry Blackstone, who by 1940 had the largest magic show on tour in America and presented full evening performances in cities from coast to coast, throughout the entire theatrical season, thus establishing himself as the fourth in the great line of Herrmann, Kellar and Thurston.

In their search for the spectacular, the great magicians began producing entire choruses of girls from a single empty cabinet. They vanished horses, automobiles and even elephants. Not content with merely levitating ladies, they vanished them while they were in midair. One vaudeville magician even made a specialty of floating a piano and the player with it. In the course of things, they introduced new styles of illusions in which girls were sawed, spiked, crushed, and even burned alive, all without the slightest harm.

Among the vaudeville illusionists whose elaborate presentations ranked them with full evening performers was the Great Leon, who condensed much of a two-hour show into thirty minutes. Another headliner was George LaFollette, who often appeared twice on a bill first as LaFollette, a quick-change-artist, then as Rush Ling Toy in an act of Chinese magic and illusions. Few persons realized that the two performers were one and the same.

This case of dual identity brought LaFollette special mention in Ripley's "Believe It or Not" and it is approached only by the instance of Chung Ling Soo, to be mentioned later in this chapter. But LaFollette, when he appeared as Rush Ling Toy, carried his double personality on to the stage itself, something probably unparalleled in the annals of magic. He still performs in both guises, though the public has now been acquainted with the fact.

To draw comparisons between the magical greats of the American stage would be difficult, not because they reached their peaks at different periods, but because of the individual characteristics that contributed to their greatness. Herrmann was noted for the air of mystery that surrounded his performances. Kellar reputedly could baffle even magicians, time and again, with certain of his tricks. Thurston's forte was the dramatic, which he carried to great intensity. Blackstone stands as inimitable in his ability to carry his work before the curtain and hold an audience spellbound with his smaller magic after the climax of a great illusion.

Only a real master of the magic art can stand the test of a full evening show over long, continued seasons. This does not in any way disparage the fine work of magicians in lesser fields, some of whom undoubtedly could have gained the highest rating if given opportunity or inclination. But the art of magic is judged by its greats and it stands by their achievements.

That fact offers a basis of comparison between the famous magicians of the American stage and the great American magicians whose fame was gained elsewhere. Most celebrated of the latter was Maurice Raymond, who circled the world seven times, carrying as many as three complete evening shows in order to play extended engagements in the capital cities of many lands. Known as the Great Raymond, he gave complete performances in nine different languages, which accounted for his popularity in the countries where he appeared during a career of more than fifty years. Raymond's friend Elbert Hubbard termed him the "King of America" in recognition of the worldwide charm of his magic and his personality.

Another American magician who presented large-scale magic on a global basis was Charles Carter, who gained much of his fame in the Orient, but seldom performed in America. In later years, Dante presented a huge magic show in South America and Europe, returning to New York just before the war. There he presented his show on Broadway and followed with an American tour. Less fortunate was the Great Nicola, whose last world tour was interrupted at Singapore, where his equipment sank with a ship that struck a mine.

On the list of the much-traveled greats was Carl Rosini, who gained fame as a vaudeville illusionist in the United States, then carried his magic through South America to win an equal reputation there. Rosini has toured other lands as well and has made a specialty of presenting Oriental mysteries before American audiences. Among the noted American magicians to visit India was Jack Gwynne, who offered huge rewards to any fakirs who could show him the mythical Rope Trick, but found no takers.

Among the Oriental feats that Rosini has mastered is the "Thumb Tie" in which he passes his tied thumbs through solid objects, letting spectators examine the knots at will. He performs this amazing illusion today, creating the same sensation as when he first introduced it to the American stage. From India, Rosini also brought the fabulous "Basket Trick" and has presented it not only on the stage but in the center of a nightclub floor, causing a boy to vanish in the very midst of an audience.

One of the most traveled magicians was Milbourne Christopher, who aptly styles himself the "Marco Polo of Magic." While in the service during World War 11, Christopher gave more than a thousand performances of magic, many of them close to the front lines in Europe. His travels have taken him to more than thirty countries, where he has presented magic in the modern trend, specializing in smaller effects which can be readily carried on long journeys, particularly by air.

The phenomenal rise of vaudeville in England, soon after the beginning of the century, attracted many magicians from the States. One was Horace Goldin who introduced a silent, rapid-fire act in which a dozen illusions were performed in nearly as many minutes. Later, Goldin branched into the full-evening field, and returning to America, devised a "Sawing a Lady" illusion that swept the vaudeville circuits so rapidly that extra units were formed to meet the demand.

Even more unusual was the career of Billy Robinson, stage manager for Herrmann the Great, who devised his own vaudeville act a few years after the maestro's death. Robinson observed that the public was much intrigued by Ching Ling Foo, a Chinese magician then touring the world. Converting his American illusions into Chinese settings, Robinson billed himself as Ching Ling Soo and was an instantaneous success. By the time the public learned that this now Chinese wonderworker was really an American, Robinson was so well established that he continued to appear as Chung Ling Soo until his death.

Another performer who sprang to fame in that lush period was Harry Houdini, whose career is something of an enigma when considered in terms of magic. Houdini set London agog over his highly publicized escape act and for some fifteen years specialized in that type of work almost exclusively. Escapes had been presented by magicians long before Houdini's time and an American performer named Brindamour was quite successful in this field at the time when Houdini began crashing headlines abroad.

Brindamour followed the Herrmann style, presenting his escapes in a polished, mystical manner; whereas Houdini turned the act into a challenge. Houdini met with strong competition which he did his utmost to drive out or discourage. Probably his greatest rival was an escape artist named Bob Cunning, who turned to other fields when escape work began to lose its sensational appeal.

During the years in which he rose to fame, Houdini was not rewarded by the public as a magician, but rather as a man of mystery who might be anything from a contortionist to a stunt artist. Done mostly in closed cabinets, escapes created great audience suspense but were puzzling more than magical. Houdini was unparalleled as a showman, but some of his magic was comparatively mediocre, a fact which must be stated in justice to the contemporary performers whose names have been mentioned.

Turning to magic after the escape field waned, Houdini presented single illusions during different seasons at the New York Hippodrome, being featured with the huge extravaganzas that appeared there. Later he entered the lecture field, attacking fraudulent mediums. Gaining tremendous publicity, he started out with his own show, presenting magic and illusions followed by a spook expose. Houdini was hardly into his second season when his untimely death occurred on October 31, 1926.

Houdini's magic show was inherited by his brother, Theo Hardeen who trimmed it to a vaudeville act and performed the choicest of its effects and illusions for nearly twenty years. Since Hardeen's death, some of the Houdini magic has been presented by his former assistant, Douglas Geoffrey, appearing as Hardeen Junior.

It was during Houdini's early surge to fame that he called upon his younger brother to adopt the name of Hardeen and fill added engagements. Presenting escapes in the same style as Houdini, Hardeen was booked solidly for years on the British vaudeville circuits. Later he returned to America and played vaudeville in friendly competition with Houdini.

Time and again, Hardeen matched Houdini's stunt of jumping handcuffed from high bridges, making his escape under water.

Both as an escape artist and a magician, Hardeen duplicated much of Houdini's work, yet today the fame of Houdini is more exaggerated than ever. From this it may be concluded that the alchemy of time can transmute gross publicity into golden legend.

Despite the grand scale performances and widespread fame of American magicians, the happy land of magic's high development has been England. For years, London had its own magical theatre, St. George's Hall, once under the joint management of Maskelyne and Devant, two names to conjure with. John Nevil Maskelyne was one of the great inventive geniuses of magic, and members of his family continued his work in the development and presentation of the art.

David Devant held top rating among British illusionists, whose names and creations would require a chapter in themselves. Some of the finest illusions which American magicians rendered famous through their performances were of British origin. In England, magicians gained great popularity on the variety stage. In that country, too, interest in amateur performances and magic as a hobby had an earlier start than in America, which accounts in no small measure for the development of new effects to please a discriminating public.

The top traveling magician of the 1990s is undoubtedly David Copperfield. He has been seen on TV and in person by more people than any other magician, living or dead. He has combined illusions with other forms of magic and staging to present his full evening show. Other top illusionists of today include Siegfried & Roy, Lance Burton, The Pendragons, and Harry Blackstone Jr.

1. Film-to-Life

Though the illusion of "Film-to-Life" has been rated as the greatest unsolved mystery of modern magic, it does not deserve such an extravagant claim. It is nevertheless a unique stage effect and captured public interest from the day it was introduced. Shown by Horace Goldin during a world tour, it was later adapted and presented by Howard Thurston during an entire season. Few other magicians have used it, due to the complications of production. As a result its secret is comparatively little known.

A movie screen about ten feet square is lowered to the stage and the magician, standing slightly to the side, introduces "Film-to-Life." A scene is projected on the screen, showing a garden; when the magician claps his hands, a girl appears in the picture, which is scaled exactly to life size. The magician bows to the girl and invites her to sit down, but she gestures that she has no chair. A clap of the magician's hands and a chair appears beside the girl in the picture, much to her amazement.

As the girl starts to sit down, she drops a handkerchief. Before she can pick it up, the magician stoops toward the screen and plucks the handkerchief right out of the picture. Showing it both to the film girl and the audience, the magician rolls the handkerchief and tosses it into the film where the girl catches it. The magician then brings out a cigarette case and offers the girl a smoke. She nods; he holds the cigarette case to the screen. The girl plucks a cigarette from the case. The magician takes one for himself.

The girl then gestures that she needs a light, so the magician flicks a lighter, holds its flame to the screen and lights the girl's cigarette. Lighting a cigarette himself, he steps to the side of the screen and suddenly arrives in the picture with the girl. There the magician performs a few magical effects and walks out again upon the stage, coming from the side of the screen. He then invites the girl to join him; stepping to the very center of the stage, he extends his hand, the girl steps forward from the film and as the stage lights suddenly come up, the girl emerges from the motion picture, which ends as she walks to the footlights holding the magician's hand.

Though the effect is intriguing throughout, its mysteries are comparatively minor until the climax. The film of course is specially photographed and later rehearsed accordingly. The plucking of the handkerchief from the film is simply clever palming on the magician's part. During the taking of the film at that point, the handkerchief was removed from the picture. Hence when the magician displays a real handkerchief that he has apparently taken from the screen, the one in the picture is gone.

Similarly, the tossing of the handkerchief into the picture—a very neat effect—is actually the vanish of a handkerchief on the magician's part, timed to the girl's catching of a handkerchief through trick photography used in the taking of the film. The proffering of a cigarette and light are also matters of timing, but this combination of real life with reel has a very baffling effect upon the audience.

The magician walks into the picture by stepping through a slit in the curtained frame that borders it at sides and top. The border looks quite solid and the darkness at the edge of the screen aids in the illusion. The magician's sudden appearance in the picture is timed so neatly that he actually appears to merge into the film. Similarly, his reappearance from the slit in the border is very effective. The sheer novelty of the whole presentation captures the imagination and has the audience believing such things happen.

The screen is affixed to two vertical rollers set in the borders at the side, like a double-ended window shade. It has a few feet of extra length which enables its center to be doubled back, forming a tuck or loop behind the center of the screen. All the while the real girl is in this upright pocket which is held in place by a row of tiny snaps. The division of title screen is not noticeable in the reduced light of the film. As the magician reaches for the film girl's hand, the cue is given; the rollers whip in opposite directions, driving the screen taut. The real girl is practically precipitated forward as the pocket straightens out. Simultaneously, bright lights come on and the magician and the actual girl are walking forward in the glare which reveals only the smooth surface of an apparently normal screen.

The cost of producing the film, the necessity of always being the same girl, and the need of the services of a motion-picture operator, plus the fact that the illusion is only for a regular theater stage—all were reasons why "Film-to-Life" belonged strictly to a large vaudeville act or a full evening magic show.

This unusual stage effect belongs more in the realm of hypnotism than magic, so far as its impression on the audience is concerned. When it was presented by Thurston, he introduced it as a demonstration of hypnosis, though the rest of his show consisted entirely of magic. It was good psychology to include such an effect, as Thurston, like other stage magicians, gave quasi-explanations of some of his illusions by attributing them to hypnotic power. Nevertheless, this particular effect could hardly be presented as anything other than a hypnotic experiment.

2. The Girl of Iron

The performer introduces a girl who he claims is a remarkable hypnotic subject. He makes a few appropriate mesmeric passes and the girl becomes rigid. As she sways, she is caught by two assistants, who place her in a chair, where she remains rigid, staring at the audience.

Lifting the girl's arm, the performer stretches it in a horizontal position, draws back her sleeve and strokes the arm to make it retain its rigidity. He does the same with the other arm, so the girl is sitting with both bare arms stretched to their full length. Then to prove the amazing strength that can be acquired by a hypnotic subject, the performer orders the two assistants to bring on stepladders, which are set at each side of the chair, behind the girl's arms.

Next, each assistant climbs a ladder and from there places one foot, then the other upon an arm of the girl. Both assistants are thus standing upon the rigid arms, without any other support, much to the amazement of the audience, for the girl bears the weight with scarcely a quiver.

After everyone is convinced that this phenomenon is actual, the assistants descend by the ladders. The performer strokes the girl's arms to relax them, awakens her with a few snaps of his fingers. The girl lowers her arms, awakens and steps forward to take a bow as though nothing unusual had happened.

In fact, the trick is nowhere as unusual as it would appear. Due to the mechanical method employed, the girl has only to act the part of a hypnotized subject.

The trick depends on the chair. It has a metal framework concealed in its stout wooden legs, with a vertical bar and a T-brace in its solid back. Metal extension rods are drawn from the T-brace, which runs across the top of the chair back. These extensions are operated in the process of setting and stroking the girl's arms. Hidden behind the girl's arms, the extension rods can not be seen, but it is upon these rods that the assistants place their weight when they apparently step to the girl's arms.

Usually each assistant carries a wooden pole which he uses to take his weight while he is stepping to the extension rods. These poles, extending down to the stage, enable the assistants to gain their balance on the rods. They let the front portions of their feet rest lightly upon the girl's arms and they are then able to lift the poles.

Afterward, the performer, standing behind the chair while he strokes the girl's arms and rearranges her sleeves, is able to push the extension rods into their original position behind the chair back. Thus the "Girl of Iron" turns out to be entirely human, the term "iron" applying only to the chair.

The Girl of Iron

3. The Drop-Away Cabinet

Though this rates as one of the most remarkable illusions ever devised, it has been performed but rarely, due to difficulties in its presentation. The effect is most ambitious. It involves the complete disappearance of a girl from a curtained cabinet that is hanging four feet above the center of the stage and surrounded by a committee from the audience. In a flash, the curtains fall, the girl is gone, and everything may be examined by the mystified spectators in whose midst it happened.

The cabinet is about seven feet tall and four feet square. Its curtains are made of a heavy material, preferably velvet. The cabinet consists of a flat top, a thin floor, connected by four upright corner rods. Near the top of this skeleton affair are horizontal rods from which the curtains are hung. When a cord is drawn, the curtains are automatically and simultaneously released.

First the girl enters the cabinet. It is then drawn upward by a chain. Not until the committee surrounds the suspended cabinet are the curtains closed. Then, at the magician's pistol shot, the curtains drop and flatten on the stage, showing the skeleton cabinet empty. The curtains are spread out to show that the girl is not concealed among them.

The method requires two traps: one in the cabinet, the other in the stage directly beneath it. The trap in the cabinet floor consists of two simple flaps that hinge downward, then are sprung back up by springs, so that they lock neatly together. The flaps, however, are not locked at the outset;

or should they be so arranged, the girl's weight is sufficient to release them.

When the girl enters the cabinet, she sets her feet apart so that she is standing on a narrow frame that surrounds the flaps. The curtains are then closed around her and at the pistol shot, the girl puts her weight on the trap and drops right through at the instant the curtains drop. At the same moment, the stage trap is opened. It too is of the downward flap variety. Properly timed, the stage trap should be opened a split-second after the girl starts her fall along with the surrounding curtains. The girl continues right through the stage and the heavy curtains, coiling as they land, cover the open stage trap.

By then the trap in the cabinet floor has sprung up and locked. There is sufficient time before the curtains are gathered for the stage trap to close upward and be bolted in place from below. Thus when the curtains are spread for examination the stage is to all appearances, solid. The trap must be finely made and disguised by its carpeting, but the magician steps over it when the curtains are gathered and the cabinet is swung forward for examination.

The problem with this illusion is the perfect timing of the traps, which demands such exactitude that few magicians have cared to perform it. If the stage trap opens too soon, it will disclose the secret; too late, the girl will stop short with the curtains and flounder the rest of the way through. Hence the illusion has only been shown under ideal conditions and after long rehearsal.

Not too many modern stages still have trap doors. A special set of stairs with a trap door is commonly used today with a trap door at its top. The assistant simply slides out the trap door in the box and into a trap door at the top of the stairs.

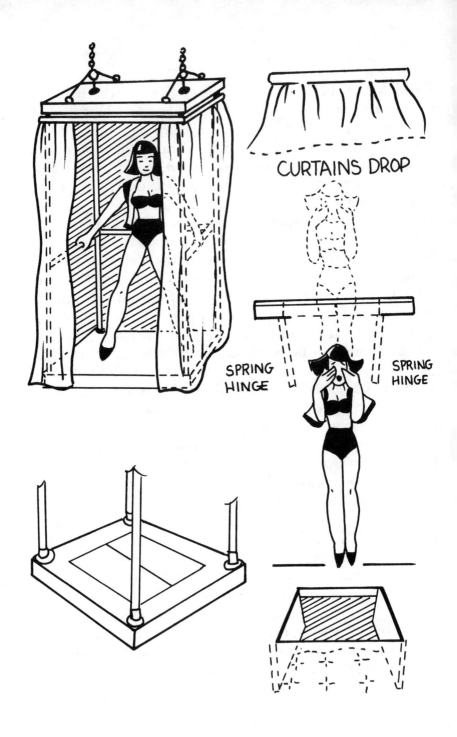

CURTAINS DROP

SPRING HINGE

SPRING HINGE

The Drop-Away Cabinet

4. The Escape from Sing Sing

This illusion combines the exciting and dramatic effects that place it in the sensational class and add much to its mystery. Originally featured by the Great Herrmann, it has been extensively copied and various other illusions have since utilized certain of its elements. Most of all it has the fast motion which blend surprise and bewilderment, where the audience is concerned.

On the stage, which is set to represent the interior of a prison, stand two large cages, resembling cells. These cells are upright, each being more than six feet high and measuring about four feet square. The cells are mounted upon platforms; their front doors are hinged. The sides of each cell are provided with roller blinds which form a bright contrast to the steel-gray bars. These blinds may be drawn down when required.

The cells are set well back and a considerable distance apart, allowing space on the center of the stage for the action which rapidly takes place. As the magician is about to introduce the illusion, a convict with striped prison uniform comes rushing on stage, brandishing a revolver. The magician grapples with him, flings him bodily into the cage on the right, clangs the door shut and pulls down the blinds.

Immediately a rattling takes place inside the cage, its front blind snaps up and instead of the convict, the audience sees a man in uniform (the warden), clamoring for release. Hardly has the magician let the warden from the cell, when a revolver shot is heard from the audience and down the aisle races the vanished convict. He rushes up on the stage, apparently seeking revenge, but this time the warden joins the magician in capturing the dangerous prisoner.

This time they put him in the cell on the left, on the assumption that he will be safer there. The blinds are pulled down on both cages and the magician, using the gun that he has wrested from the convict, tops off the drama with sheer wizardry. He fires at the cell on the left, its curtains are released, and again the convict has vanished. The curtains are released around the cell on the right and the convict has mysteriously arrived there. Releasing the bewildered prisoner, the magician turns him over to the warden, who marches him off stage while the magician steps forward to take a bow.

One warden, two convicts, and a pair of special cells are the requirements for this illusion. The cells have loose upright bars at the back which can be quickly removed and replaced. These are masked by special curtains of the same gray as the cell bars and the prison scene. Looking through the front bars of the cell, the audience cannot detect that the back is actually solid (curtained), because so many bars intervene.

The warden is planted behind the cell at the right, where he stands on the ledge of the platform. The first convict rushes on stage, is hurriedly shoved into the cell by the magician. As soon as the curtains are lowered, the convict changes places with the warden, who immediately begins rattling the bars for release. Before the audience can guess where the convict went, his double comes charging down the aisle.

Supposedly the first convict, this man is placed in the cell on the left, where he goes through to the back the moment the curtains are drawn and is hidden there, when they fly up again. Meanwhile, the first convict steps into the cell on the right and appears there when the curtains are raised.

The speed of action and the conspicuous costume of the convict draws suspicion from the fact that doubles are used. The intersection of the warden as a character in the scene is an added factor that does much to confuse the audience. This illusion, however, requires precision as well as rapidity to make it a strong mystery.

The double who appears in the audience goes around to the front of the theater just about the time the illusion begins, rather than be seen there early. Once when Billy Robinson (later Chung Ling Soo) was playing the duplicate convict for Herrmann, he was a trifle late and had to rush to get to the front of the house. On the way, he was spotted by a passing patrolman who mistook him for a real convict, arrested him and put him in jail. During that show, the "convict" never did reappear from the audience and was not located until the next morning.

Blackstone experienced a similar episode when performing an illusion in which an assistant did a quick "run around" and came in from the audience. His assistant mistook the lobby of a movie house for Blackstone's theater, burst into an audience that was watching a Western picture, fired a gun three times and shouted "Here I am!" That took a lot of explanation, but the assistant finally was guided to the right theater, where he made a much belated reappearance.

5. Spiked Alive

A girl stands in an upright cabinet, large enough to receive her comfortably but with comparatively little room to spare. Above the girl is a square block of wood, from which dozens of long spikes project downward. This block has four handles, two to a side, projecting through slits cut in the opposite sides of the cabinet.

The door of the cabinet is closed and two brawny assistants seize the projecting handles of the spiked block. Slowly they draw the handles downward, clear to the bottom of the cabinet, where the spikes make their appearance through the floor of the platform on which the cabinet stands. Apparently the spikes have completely penetrated the hapless girl, but when the spiked block is shoved up to the top of the cabinet again, the door opens and the girl steps out, smiling, at her terrible experience.

This is a very convincing illusion because the spiked block can be slid up and down beforehand to show that it actually operates in formidable fashion. Furthermore, a ribbon can be tied to one of the spikes and the ribbon will come out through the platform, proving that it is the same spike. Nevertheless, all such mysteries have a solution and this one, though deceptive, is comparatively simple.

The whole center of the block is a separate square that simply fits in the outer rim, or frame. This square stays in place by its own weight, its sides being cut at a slightly inward angle. Thus the whole block moves up and down under ordinary conditions, but when the girl is in the cabinet, she has only to place her hands between the center spikes and hold the center of the block, whereupon only the outer frame and its row of spikes will descend when the handles are drawn downward.

The frame is large enough to go around the girl. When it reaches the bottom of the cabinet, its spikes come out through holes in the platform. In the platform is a thin square of metal or wood, provided with spires to account for those in the center of the block. This square is held up by springs inside the platform, which has a double bottom.

Tiny posts or flanges inside the cabinet, at the corners, are engaged by the descending frame. These control the slab hidden in the platform, with its short spikes. Thus the secret slab descends with the frame and pushes the proper number of extra spikes into sight below the platform. When the frame is pushed upward, the hidden square rises with it, bringing the fake spikes up into the platform. The assistants continue upward with the frame and when it reaches the top of the cabinet, it gathers the spiked square that the girl is holding there. This brings everything back to its original status.

The business of the ribbon attached to a spike is simply explained by the fact that it is tied to one of the spikes in the outer frame, hence it actually comes down through the platform with the spike.

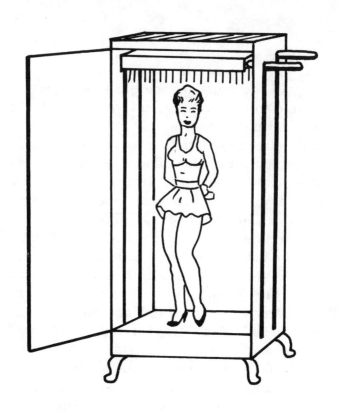

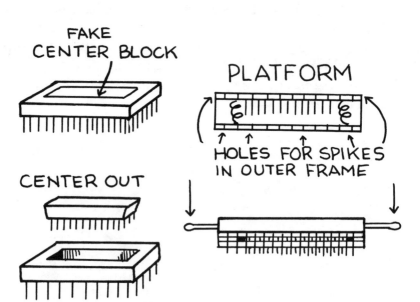

FAKE
CENTER BLOCK

PLATFORM

HOLES FOR SPIKES
IN OUTER FRAME

CENTER OUT

Spiked Alive

6. The Glass Sheet Mystery

Originally planned by Houdini, this illusion was never presented in his show, but later it was built and successfully performed, exactly as designed. Though in effect it is another form of a "Vanishing Lady" illusion, this mystery meets the most exacting conditions. Not only is the girl vanished from a sheet of plate glass; it can be done with the audience on all sides and even performed "in the middle of a thoroughfare" as Houdini himself specified to the author of this book.

The effect is this: Four assistants clad in Oriental regalia are holding a sheet of plate glass. All the assistants are facing the same direction; two at the front corners, two at the back. The girl is placed on the sheet of glass, which is held flat; a cloth is spread over her by the magician. Suddenly, the magician whisks the cloth away and the girl is gone.

Immediately the four Oriental assistants march away with the sheet of glass, leaving only an empty cloth and a much perplexed audience.

The illusion itself is quite ingenious and worthy of the claims made for it, though if performed out of doors, the setting would have to be arranged beforehand. The cloth used must be a large one, so that it drapes well over the sides of the glass, which is just about long enough to receive the girl. Ordinarily, the magician and an assistant simply spread the cloth full width before draping it over the girl; but if observers are on all sides, the cloth must be specially prepared to retain its shape while the girl is making a quick departure.

That still leaves the question: Where does the girl go? The answer involves the Oriental assistants, in particular one of them, who really doesn't exist. Of the four assistants, only three are real. The fourth, the figure standing at the front of the glass on the side away from the audience, is a dummy figure, entirely hollow. This is the reason for the Oriental regalia, aided by bearded faces, so the dummy looks precisely like the three real assistants.

The back of the dummy figure is open, hidden by the loose-fitting tunic which the figure wears. As soon as the girl is hidden by the cloth, she works her way feet first down into the dummy figure, raising the back of the tunic so she can work her head and shoulders up into the dummy.

There is no reason for the girl to slide her hand down into the dummy's arm, for the figure is attached to the glass sheet and the real assistant at the front is holding up the glass. But as soon as the girl is standing in the dummy's legs, the magician yanks away the cloth and the Oriental assistant's depart, the girl walking off inside the dummy.

A slow, impressive march and the effect is perfect. The dummy now is real, so far as its action is concerned and can not be distinguished from the genuine assistant's. Having no reason to suspect that one of the glass carriers is a dummy, the audience is thoroughly baffled by the girl's mysterious disappearance.

7. Crushing A Girl

Introduced by Thurston, this illusion belongs in the "torture" class of stage magic. On a raised platform stands an oblong box with two doors that are lowered in the front, spaced several inches apart. This box, which has no top, is more than large enough to hold a girl, who enters the box and reclines there. In with the girl are placed a dozen inflated toy balloons, which serve a surprising purpose later.

Another box is introduced, slightly smaller than the first. This oblong box likewise has two front doors; also a similar pair of doors in its top. Thus it resembles two square boxes fashioned into one. Two girls enter this box, one in each side, from the top. The front doors are opened, showing the girls in seated positions, due to the limited size of the compartments. The front doors of this box are closed, but the top doors remain open or are removed, because the heads and shoulders of the girls emerge from the top of the box.

The box containing the two girls is hoisted by chains until it hovers above the larger box that holds the reclining girl. The doors of the larger box are closed. Then, slowly, impressively, the chains are released so that the smaller box, with its double weight, descends into the lower, threatening the welfare of the girl reposing therein.

Since she has no way of escape, the girl in the lower box is threatened by a crushing doom. This becomes more imminent as the upper box sinks 'into the lower. Proving that the fateful moment is nigh, balloons begin to burst, muffled but audibly, until the smaller box has settled entirely within the lower, completely filling it.

Assistants open the front doors of the boxes. Inside are seen the two girls seated in the smaller box. The girl who occupied the lower box is gone; by magician's logic she has been crushed between the floors of the two boxes. The doors are closed again, the smaller box is hoisted from the larger. When the doors are reopened, there is the girl reclining as calmly as ever, thoroughly recuperated from her crushing experience.

This illusion is accomplished through an ingenious construction of the upper box. Its two sections are divided by a pair of partitions, with a space between, running from front to back of the box. These partitions are like side walls of each section, very close to the edge of each door. However, the partitions are not seen, because the girls are in the box when the doors are opened and they crowd over, hiding the walls beside them.

The space between the partitions is bottomless. Hence the girl in the lower box has only to take a position on hands and knees, facing forward in the exact center of the box; then, when the upper box descends, the hollow space slides over the girl, its walls and top surrounding her like a shell.

The girl lets the balloons remain loose; hence they pop as the smaller box settles into place, giving the "crushing" an authentic touch. After the doors of the boxes have been opened, closed, and the smaller box hoisted, the girl in the larger box resumes her reclining position, giving the impression that she almost fills the box, thus minimizing the size of the space in which she was temporarily crouched.

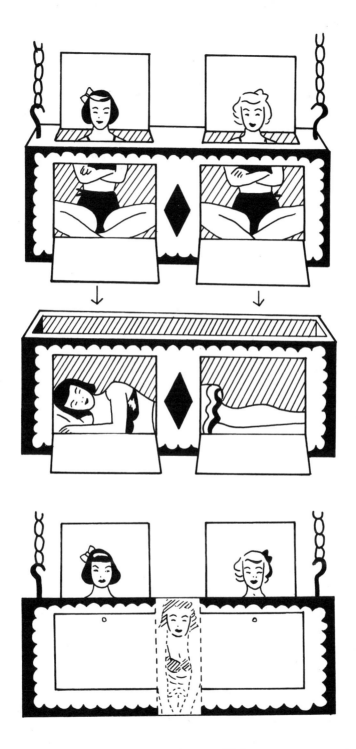

Crushing a Girl

8. The Cane Cabinet

Both baffling and convincing, this illusion forms an interesting variation from the usual form of "torture tricks" in which a young lady proves herself impervious to sinister methods designed for her destruction.

On the stage is a cabinet mounted on a thin platform so that everyone can see beneath it. The cabinet consists simply of two doors, front and back, side walls and a hinged top that opens upward. Doors and sides are bored with holes, set at regular intervals, in rows.

A young lady enters the cabinet and fills it rather plentifully. The doors are closed, the cabinet is wheeled around, and the magician and his assistants then begin to thrust long canes through the doors and walls of the cabinet, the ends of the canes emerging from the opposite door or side.

Dozens of canes are used, the exact number being immaterial, except that the canes must be abundant enough to prove that the girl cannot possibly squeeze between them. Hence when canes have been thrust through all the holes, the cabinet fairly bristles with the walking sticks, convincing all the spectators that there is not as much as a square foot of space in which the girl could compress herself. The only answer therefore is that a considerable number of the canes must have been thrust through the girl's body.

Then comes the question of the girl's welfare or survival, which the magician promptly settles to the satisfaction of the breathless audience. The canes are all pulled away and flung to the floor. A door of the cabinet is opened and the girl steps out, quite unharmed. Or if the magician prefers to make the climax of the illusion more rapid, a rope can be let down from above, the top of the cabinet opened, and the girl drawn upward clinging to the rope, thus coming clear of all the penetrating canes.

The cane cabinet is a most ingenious device, its great feature being its complete lack of all complications. The canes are genuine and there is no trick whatever about the cabinet itself. The top is of ornamental construction, taking up some six inches or more of space, which looks trivial in proportion to the full height of the cabinet. Furthermore, the uppermost row of holes is several inches below the top proper. Thus the girl can cram herself safely in the least suspected portion of the cabinet, the top.

How does the girl reach the top? The answer discloses the full ingenuity of the illusion. The canes are all thrust into the cabinet in regular order, starting from the bottom and going upward. All the girl does is climb the canes as she would a ladder, pressing her hands against the sides of the cabinet to steady her ascent. By the time the final canes are thrust through the holes, the girl is compactly perched in her unsuspected hiding place.

If the canes are removed so that the girl can step from the door, she has only to descend while the canes are being pulled out from the top of the cabinet to the bottom. If the girl is hauled out by a rope, she simply comes up head and shoulders first. In this case, the hinged top should swing toward the audience, so that spectators in a balcony cannot look into the cabinet while the girl emerges.

9. Catching A Bullet

This celebrated mystery has been performed by a variety of methods, any of which may prove fatal. In nearly every version, the effect is essentially the same. A bullet is marked, then loaded into a gun which is fired point-blank at the magician, who is holding a plate in front of him. The magician coolly catches the bullet between his teeth, drops it on the plate and extends it to the man who marked the bullet, so that it can be identified.

In an obscure book on magic compiled shortly before the year 1800, Philip Astley of London credits himself with the invention of "Bullet Catching," claiming that he devised it in order that a foolish duel between two British army officers would be taught with blank guns. Yet in the years that followed, more than a dozen fatal accidents were recorded among magicians whose precautions failed them during the performance of the trick.

Professor Anderson, the Scottish magician who styled himself the "Wizard of the North" a century ago, performed the trick perhaps a few thousand tines without experiencing harm. His playbills term it "The Gun Delusion" and challenge the audience in so many words to "Bring your own gun." One of Anderson's methods was to switch the marked bullet for an amalgam imitation which dissipated itself when fired from the gun. Once, it is said, a spectator refused to let Anderson handle the bullet and loaded the genuine article in the gun. Anderson challenged him to go ahead and fire, figuring that the man knew the secret and would lose his nerve, which he did.

Considering the fatalities that had occurred with other magicians, the Wizard was taking a long chance on that occasion, trusting in a spectator's whim. Herrmann the Great, who performed the "Bullet Catching" a generation or more later, left the actual shooting to a group of his assistants who appeared as a squad of soldiers. Several bullets were marked, then switched by the captain of the squad, cartridges and all. The bullets fired were of wax and while the squad was lining up, Herrmann obtained the real bullets which were extracted from the cartridges offstage.

The Herrmann presentation was highly spectacular, for on occasion he had the firing squad stand on a platform over the center of the audience, aiming their rifles at the magician on the stage. Though the friendly marksmen never scored a hit on Herrmann, the method was not foolproof enough for his chief assistant, Billy Robinson, who later became the pretended Chinese magician, Chung Ling Soo. Robinson used an old muzzle-loading rifle which had been converted to the breech-loading type. The real bullet dropped down through the breech into the disused ramrod barrel and the magician caught a duplicate. In 1918, when Robinson was performing in Chinese costume on the stage of a London variety theater, the charge fired both barrels and he was killed.

The preferred method of "Bullet Catching" is a one-man version which can be worked anywhere. The secret is little known because so few magicians have been willing to risk its performance and it seems well established that even Houdini, though noted for his daredevil challenges, avoided the bullet trick. The trick is worked with an old-fashioned muzzle-loading pistol which can be fired by a percussion cap and is presented as follows:

The magician gives a bullet to be marked, preferably with knife-scratches. He lets the pistol be examined, then pours a charge of powder into its muzzle. Next, paper wadding is inserted and tamped down with a short, ornamental ram-rod the size of the gun barrel. The ramrod is decorated with circular grooves that appear at regular intervals around its circumference.

In his hand, the magician has a short tube, open at one end, which exactly matches the metal of the ramrod. After letting some person tamp down the powder wadding, the magician takes the pistol by the muzzle and with the handle pointing down, he secretly drops the little tube into the gun, so that it lands with its opening upward. The bullet is next dropped into the muzzle and it falls into the tube. Taking the ramrod, the magician goes through the motions of ramming the bullet home. Actually, the ramrod picks up the tube, which stops even with the first concentric circle.

Thus the bullet is extracted with the ramrod, which has gained a few inches in length, though this is never noticed. The magician now uses the other end of the ramrod to tamp home another supply of wadding. Leaving the gun in a spectator's possession, the magician takes his distance of say twenty paces, carrying the ramrod with him. While his back is turned, he pulls the tube from the end of the ramrod, obtains the bullet and slips it in his mouth while stooping to pick up a plate from a table. Pocketing the little metal tube, he holds the plate in front of him, faces the gun, and orders the spectator to fire it. There is a report, the magician shows the bullet between his teeth, and the trick is as good as finished.

Not only does this method dispense with assistants who might become careless; the performer faces a gun that has a blank charge and can check the fact because he has extracted the bullet. If for any reason the little tube should prove empty, the magician can call off the trick. Nevertheless, the method is not foolproof. There is still a chance that somebody might drop some other missive into the pistol. On this account, some performers have used an assistant to handle and fire the gun after it has presumably been loaded.

Because of its danger—or at least the threat of such—"Bullet Catching" is scarcely ever performed today. It has been done on special occasions using a model rifle, with firearms identification experts present to confirm the markings on the bullet. But the jinx that holds over it has caused professional magicians to become too wary to include the "Bullet Catching" illusion in their regular performances.

This trick is not recommended for anyone to perform, amateur or professional.

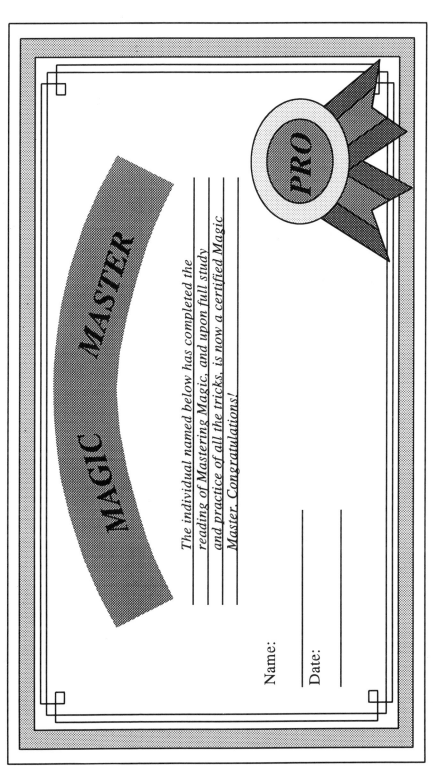

MAGIC MASTER

PRO

The individual named below has completed the reading of Mastering Magic, and upon full study and practice of all the tricks, is now a certified Magic Master. Congratulations!

Name: _____

Date: _____

Magic Shops

A.J. WORLD OF MAGIC & FUN
3115 Shadow Walk Lane
Tucker, GA 30084
404-491-8245

AL'S MAGIC SHOP
1012 Vermont Ave. NW
Washington, DC 20005-4901
202-789-2800

AMAZING BECKMAN
1501 Pike Pl.
Seattle, WA 98101
206-624-3271

ANNIES COSTUME & MAGIC
801 S. University B136
Plantation, FL 33324
305-432-3606

BALI MAGIC
545 Main 215
E Dundee, IL 60118

BEN'Z MAGIC SHOP
4552 Kirkwood Drive
Sterling Heights, MI 48310
313-526-2442

BENZ MAGIC SHOP
P.P. Box 05010
Detroit, MI 48206
313-526-2442

BISHOP'S MAGIC SHOP
3242 Harlmen Ave.
Riverside, IL 60546-2069
708-442-9166

BJ'S MAGIC
118-20 14th Rd.
College Point, NY 11356
718-353-5648

C & M PRODUCTIONS
4136 N 37th Stl.
Tacoma, WA 98407
206-752-8158

CALLIN NOVELTIES
412 SW 4th Ave.
Portland, OR 97204-2202
503-223-4821

CAMIRAND ACADEMY
OF MAGIC, INC.
Succ. A, P.O. Box 269
Longueuil, PQ J4H 3X6 Canada
514-670-6026

CENTER STAGE
4910A Hwy. 17S at Carousel
N. Myrtle Beach, SC 29582
803-272-4227

CHUCK HAYES MAGIC
PRODUCTIONS
103 Bleeker Rd. Apt. 11
Guilderland, NY 12084-9667
518-869-3315

CHUCK'S HOUSE OF MAGIC
150 W. Joe Orr Rd.
Chicago Hts., IL 60411
708-754-2111

CLOWN ANTICS
38092 Hixford Pl.
Westland, MI 48185-3393
313-721-3970

CLOWN CITY
1 Inchcliffe Dr.
Gales Ferry, CT 06335-1807
203-464-7116

CROWN MAGIC & FUN SHOP
4202 E. 10 Mile Rd.
Warren, MI 48091-1577
313-755-9181

DAYTONA MAGIC
136 S. Beach St.
Daytona Beach, FL 32114-4402
904-252-6767
904-252-9037

DELBEN MAGIC, INC.
P.O. Box 1835
Spring, TX 77383
713-353-6618

DON'S MAGIC & FUN SHOP
1901 Estero Blvd. - #8
Ft. Myers Beach, FL 33931
813-463-7005

EDDIE'S TRICK & NOVELTY
SHOP, INC.
262 Rio Circle
Decatur, GA 30030
404-377-0003

ELBEE CO.
520 Broadway St.
SanAntonio, TX 78215
210-223-4561
210-226-9185

ELMWOOD MAGIC &
NOVELTY
507 Elmwood Ave.
Buffalo, NY 14222
716-886-5653

FANTASTIC MAGIC
COMPANY
P.O. Box 33156
Granada Hills, CA 91394-3156
805-252-1142
805-252-1186

FEDKO MAGIC COMPANY
13111 Flint Dr.
Santa Ana, CA 92705-1859
714-538-6044

FRANKEL'S COSTUME
4815 Fannin St.
Houston, TX 77004-5699
713-528-6036

GOLDEN'S MAGIC WAND
P.O. Box 1509
San Marcos, CA 92079-1509
619-471-0100
619-756-0820

GUARANTEED MAGIC
27 Bright Rd.
Hatboro, PA 19040-2023
215-672-3344
215-674-2826

HANK LEE'S MAGIC
FACTORY
P.O. Box 789
Medford, MA 02155-0006
617-391-8749
617-395-2034

HOLLYWOOD MAGIC, INC.
6614 Hollywood Blvd.
Hollywood, CA 90028
213-464-5610

HOUSE OF MAGIC
2025 Chestnut St.
San Francisco, CA 94123-2701
415-346-2218

HUGHES MAGIC
352 N. Prospect St.
Ravenna, OH 44266
216-296-4023

JACK MILLER ENTERPRISES
1317 Shawn Dr.
Seneca Falls, NY 13148-9780
315-568-8721

JOES HOUSE OF MAGIC
2 Stanton Blvd.
Uniondale, NY 11583

KARDWELL
INTERNATIONAL, INC.
P.O. Box 775
Orient, NY 11957-0775
800-233-0828
516-323-3904

KARTAY'S HOUSE OF MAGIC
14-A Braddock Square
LaVale, MD 21502
301-729-3971

KOGEL'S MAGIC
6751 Colbert St.
New Orleans, LA 70124-2240
504-482-5153

LA MAISON DE LA MAGIE
4263 St. Hubert St.
Montreal PQ H2J 2W6 Canada
514-935-6244

LEE JACOBS PRODUCTS
P.O. Box 362
Pomeroy, OH 45769-0362
614-992-5208

LOUIS TANNEN, INC.
6 W 32nd St. Fl. 4th
New York, NY 10001-3867
212-239-8383

MAGIC HOUSE OF
BABCOCK
3755 Eels Rd.
Cashmere, WA 98815-9745
509-782-2730

MAGIC INDUSTRIES, INC.
3309 Broad Rock Blvd.
Richmond, VA 23224
804-230-1500

MAGIC SHOP
P.O. Box 1307
Pigeon Forge, TN 37863

MAGIC SHOP OF RENO
1 North Virginia
Reno, NV 89501
702-786-6544

MAGICAL MYSTERIES
4700 N. 31 Ct.
Hollywood, FL 33021
305-987-1039

MAGIC TRICKS & BOOKS
20702 Reef Ln.
Huntington Beach, CA
92646-6554
714-962-7087

MAGIC WORLD
327 Clay St.
Milltown, NJ 08850-1445
201-545-9624

MAGIC, INC.
5082 N. Lincoln Ave.
Chicago, IL 60625-2692

MAGICAL PRODUCTIONS
INTERNATIONAL
1020 N 4th St.
Berthoud, CO 80513-1121
303-532-0350
303-532-0347

MARCELO CONTENTO
P.O. Box 792
Boston, MA 02123-0792
617-262-1050

MARKET MAGIC SHOP
1501 Pike Pl. #427
Seattle, WA 98101-1542
206-624-4271
206-624-4919

MECCA MAGIC
49 Dodd St.
Bloomfield, NJ 07003

MERLIN'S MYSTICAL
EMPORIUM
363 South Mills #1650
Ventura, CA 93003
805-639-0044

MOSTLY MAGIC SHOP
311 D. Street
Santa Rosa, CA 95404
707-523-2842

MR. G'S
1708 Park Ave. Hwy. 17
Orange Park, FL 32073
904-269-6791

MR. MAGIC
1917 North Grant
Little Rock, AR
501-666-8735

MR. E'S MAGIC &
NOVELTIES
314-A E Pershing St.
Springfield, MO 65806
417-862-1968

MYSTIC MARTY'S MAGIC
MAD HOUSE
10 Dundar Rd.
Edison, NJ 08817

NUMO MANUFACTURING
CO., INC.
700 Hickory Tree Rd.
Mesquite, TX 75149-3914
214-288-4423

OASIS MAGIC
5723 N. Sultana Ave.
Temple City, CA 91780-2334
818-286-6412

PERFECT MAGIC
4781 Van Horne Ave. - #206
Montreal PQ H3W 1J1 Canada
514-738-4176
514-738-9738

RABBIT IN THE HAT RANCH
1017 Crystal Bowl Circle
Casselberry, FL 32707-4536
407-695-3630

SHOWPLACE NOVELTY
AND MAGIC
50 S. Main St. Ste. 92
Salt Lake City, UT 84144-2019
801-359-3349

SPECTRAM MAGIC
1237 Jean-Talon Est.
Montreal PQ H2R 1W1 Canada
514-495-2312
514-270-7817

STERLING MAGIC
MANUFACTURING
30998 Huntwood Ave. Ste. 103
Hayward, CA 94544-7033
510-487-6391
510-471-0249

STEVENS' MAGIC EMPORIUM
3238 E. Douglas Ave.
Wichita, KS 67208-3396
316-683-9582
316-686-2442

STONER'S FUNSTORES
712 S. Harrison St.
Ft. Wayne, IN 46802
219-743-4908

SUDS' MAGIC
24795 Heil Dr.
Moreno Valley, CA 92553-5878
909-242-8376

TAKESHI NEMOTO
505 B 17-3
Yamate-Cho Suita-Shi
Osaka, Japan

TANNENS MAGIC
24 West 25th St. 2nd Floor
New York City, NY 10010
212-929-4565

THE MAGIC CONNECTION
6663 Huntley Road Ste. F
Columbus, OH 43229
414-848-8749

TONY'S TRICK AND
JOKE SHOP
532 Broughton St.
Victoria BC V8W 1C6 Canada
604-385-6807
604-385-5543

TOP HAT MAGIC
5555 E 41st St.
Tulsa, OK 74135-6008
918-663-5550
918-663-6258

TWIN CITIES MAGIC &
COSTUME CO.
241 West 7th St.
St. Paul, MN 55102
612-227-7888

THE MAGIC BASEMENT
2790 Mooring Ct. #105
Lantana, FL 33462

WINKLER'S WAREHOUSE
OF WONDERS
24 Doyle Rd.
Oakdale, CT 06370-1052
203-859-3474

WIZARDZ
1000 Universal Center Drive
Citywalk 217
Universal City, CA 91608
818-506-0066

WORLD OF MAGIC
P.O. Box 584
Green River, UT 84525-0584
800-771-7012